More Praise for

NET WORK

"A backstage pass to a part of the NBA that most fans never see . . . For anyone looking to play at the elite level—or just admire those who do—this book delivers the secrets of how to both arrive and thrive."

—Pete Thamel, senior writer at Yahoo! Sports

"McClanaghan inspires many at all levels of the game to learn from him. His training has never been about gimmicks and neither is this book. Rather, it is filled with the elusive truths that can only be gleaned by being a lifelong student of the game."

—Jim Boeheim, men's basketball coach,
Syracuse University

"If someone is serious, and I mean serious—not just saying the right thing, but serious—about taking their game to the next level, they work with Rob Mac. I've seen it for years with dozens of guys around the league. There's a reason he's in such high demand all the time, year after year. It's a system, and that's hard to beat."

—Gunnar Peterson CSCS, director of strength
and endurance, Los Angeles Lakers

"In the basketball world that existed twenty years ago, the position of 24/7 on-call trainer didn't exist, which makes Rob McClanaghan's journey—compellingly told here along with that of his superstar clients—all the more remarkable. He wasn't the first to try working with players in a hyper-focused way, but in doing so he set a new standard. Ultimately, what this book has to say about players applies equally to McClanaghan: only sustained, brutally hard work, and a determination to attack weaknesses, will result in all-world performance."

—Sonny Vaccaro, former sports marketer for Nike, Adidas,
and Reebok and founder of ABCD All-America Camp

"It's no secret why Rob has been so continuously successful with such high-level athletes. The trust that he has developed not only on the court, grinding it out with them day in and day out, but off the court with their development as people speaks for itself. He's authentic in everything he does, and this book is a testament to the reputation that he has established during his career."

—Mike Hopkins, men's basketball coach,
University of Washington

"It's not the game—it's the game plan. In *Net Work*, one of the most engaging recent books about what it takes to dominate in the NBA, Rob drives home the point that playing games is hard work and serious business!"

—Brandon Steiner, CEO of Steiner Sports

NET WORK

TRAINING THE NBA'S BEST
AND FINDING THE KEYS TO GREATNESS

ROB McCLANAGHAN

SCRIBNER

NEW YORK   LONDON   TORONTO   SYDNEY   NEW DELHI

Scribner

An Imprint of Simon & Schuster, Inc.

1230 Avenue of the Americas

New York, NY 10020

First Scribner hardcover edition October 2019

SCRIBNER and design are registered trademarks of The Gale Group, Inc.,
used under license by Simon & Schuster, Inc., the publisher of this work.

For information about special discounts for bulk purchases,
please contact Simon & Schuster Special Sales at 1-866-506-1949
or business@simonandschuster.com.

The Simon & Schuster Speakers Bureau can bring authors to
your live event. For more information or to book an event,
contact the Simon & Schuster Speakers Bureau at 1-866-248-3049
or visit our website at www.simonspeakers.com.

Interior design by Kyle Kabel

Manufactured in the United States of America

1   3   5   7   9   10   8   6   4   2

Library of Congress Cataloging-in-Publication Data is available.

ISBN 978-1-9821-1479-4
ISBN 978-1-9821-1481-7 (ebook)

For my favorite players, Ela, Gia, and Rob V.
Because you make me realize what truly matters.
May all your dreams come true.

CONTENTS

FOREWORD BY STEPHEN CURRY

I first started working out with Rob McClanaghan in the summer of 2012. I'd worked with other trainers before, but, back then, I was in Los Angeles and looking to maybe bring a little extra to my preparation. Right away, I found Rob's approach appealingly different. Most trainers break down your fundamentals, and Rob did some of that, but his focus seemed to be on creating an environment that mimics what happens in an NBA game. He didn't use science and gimmicks as much as he went by feel. And the whole thing was very fast paced. Believe me, I got tired real quick.

I thought it was pretty hilarious at first. Here's this guy, hair slicked back, looking real put-together. The furthest he ever got as a player was as a walk-on at Syracuse, but he's jumping right into the drills, guarding me, talking trash, cracking jokes. He had a way of appealing to the competitor in me as well. When we got to the end of a drill, he'd start counting down "three . . . two . . . one . . ." If I missed the shot, I'd get real ticked off and want to go again. He knew how to push my buttons, that's for sure.

That was the start of a great relationship. I've worked with Rob ever since.

Technically, he works for *me*, but as is the case with all of his clients, we've become really good buddies. I'm not surprised that Rob has become one of the top trainers of players in our league. He knows basketball, but mostly he gets people. He loves the game and truly respects players of all talents. He never makes it about *him*. He genuinely cares for his clients and enjoys seeing them get better. That's not something you can fake.

Rob's workouts have a nice flow to them. He's always building your confidence. Before you know it, you're halfway through and you've made a bunch of shots in a row, and you're thinking, *This guy knows what he's doing*. What he's *really* doing, though, is giving the player an environment where he actually enjoys working and getting better. Rob's always mixing things up to keep the workout from getting stale. The feeling that it's all drudgery is a hazard players need to avoid. It's especially difficult to do that during the middle of the summer.

I've continued to work with Rob during the off-seasons, but I've also brought him with me to do clinics in three different tours through Asia. Believe me, you don't stick a guy next to you on all those long plane flights—and spend all that extended time together in a foreign country—if you don't really, *really* like him. Like me, Rob grew up in the game of basketball. He takes his work seriously but never himself. We've spent a lot of time talking ball, but we also talked about life, family, movies, whatever. It's to the point now where we have all these inside jokes, so if one of us lets slip the right words we're both cracking up. Rob's one of the funniest people I've ever met.

When it comes time to do net work, however, Rob knows how to get down to business. And he doesn't let me slide, even if I want to. During the summer of 2017, I brought him to London, where I was mostly enjoying some down time with my wife while she was doing some work. We were working out at a really no-frills gym, which wasn't a big deal because it was basically a vacation for me. One day, I was supposed to meet Rob for a workout and didn't really feel like it, so I sent him a text saying I wanted to bail. He wasn't having it. He reminded me that those are the little, off-the-radar, make-or-break moments that can make a big difference. He basically guilted me into going through with it. I knew he was right so I agreed to meet him, but I wasn't all that enthusiastic. Once he coaxed me into the gym, though, Rob got me going, just like he always does. He knows me better than I know myself sometimes.

Rob works as hard as any NBA player I know. Many times I've finished a really intense workout with him, and as I've prepared to leave the gym exhausted I've thought, *Hey, I get to leave, but Rob's going to be in the gym for the rest of the day.* That reality has made me respect him even more. Rob's not going as hard as the players, of course, but he's bringing the energy every time. I don't know if I could keep that up day after day.

Guys around the league ask me all the time whether they should work with Rob, and I tell them the same thing. If you're willing to commit to him, he will commit to you. You don't have to stress about having a big audience at your workout. He'll keep it on the down low. You'll be challenged, you'll be pushed. Best of all, you'll laugh a lot. I think it's great that Rob is enjoying so much success because he deserves it.

I'm really glad Rob decided to write this book, too. This is his way of sharing with everyone what he's learned. In the pages ahead, you're going to learn a lot about who Rob is, how he got to this point, and how he trains the very best competitors. But you're also going to get a feel for his character, his humility, his work ethic, and most of all, his sense of humor.

I feel very lucky that Rob and I have been able to do so much net work together. I'm *especially* lucky to call him my friend.

CHAPTER ONE

PERFECT REPS

It's another sunny, beautiful morning in Santa Monica, California. I'm behind the wheel of my car, circling the block near Saint Monica Catholic High School in search of a parking spot. The 9:00 a.m. workout doesn't begin for another twenty minutes, so I'm good. Or so I think.

My cell phone rings. It's Russell Westbrook. "Yo, Mac, where you at?" he says, already irritated.

"I'm parking," I say. "Don't worry, man, I'll be there. It's only eight-forty."

"Don't be late." He hangs up.

That guy's crazy, I think, not for the first time. I park and hustle into the gym. Russ has already worked up a sweat and he's ready to go. "Where are the other guys?" he asks.

"They'll be here," I say.

"They better not be late."

Pretty soon the other guys—Derrick Rose and Kevin Love—hustle into the gym. It doesn't take long for them to stretch and get ready, too, and the net work begins. We start with some basic moves—jab step right, jab step left, one-dribble pull-ups, right side, left side, pump-fake drives—with some hard sprinting in between. When they're in the NBA, these guys are competitors, but today they're . . . well, competitors. That's why the three of them like working out together.

The energy they bring is contagious. Most days it starts with Russ—that guy's got stupid intensity—but Kevin and Derrick will never let him get too far out in front, whether it's how many jumpers he makes or how hard he dunks.

After a while we graduate to more challenging moves. Pump-fake two-dribble pull-up. Jab step, crossover, drive to the rim. A series of shooting drills where they run across the court to five different spots behind the three-point line, and then catch and shoot. They attempt ten in a row and then do a sprint to the far baseline and back. They're breathing heavily, but I won't let them stop, and they don't want to show weakness. Especially if I'm keeping score.

It's the summer of 2009. All three guys are coming off rookie seasons. They were all top five picks in the draft. They played well that first year, but they're just kids—not even old enough to drink yet. They know they need to get better. That's why they're here.

And why, you may ask, am I here, a six-foot-one, 170-pound, thirty-year-old dude from Rhode Island whose only hope of getting near the floor of an NBA game is by scoring a courtside ticket? Well, I'm the trainer, which makes me the boss, I guess. Except they're also paying me (or their agents are), which also makes me their employee. I jump in and participate in the workouts, sometimes joining games of two-on-two or full-court pickup, so in a way I'm their peer (just shorter, slower, and much less talented). Often, when the workouts are done, we go to lunch or dinner, which makes us friends. And I like to stay in touch with them during the season to talk about their progress and what I'm seeing on video. So I'm kind of a coach. We talk on the phone a lot. I know they need to vent to someone, so I'm there to listen to their stresses and hear out their frustrations and insecurities. Kind of like a therapist.

This is the job of a full-time basketball trainer, a rapidly growing occupation that didn't really exist back then, at least not in the NBA. At the time, I was employed by Wasserman Media Group, an agency that represents dozens of top NBA players. There were plenty of agencies doing business, but at that time Wasserman was the most prominent for one reason—Arn Tellem. He was a real trailblazer, not only as a basketball agent but for Major League Baseball players as well. Wasserman had hired me as an extra service for their clients. It was a great part of their sales pitch—sign with Wasserman, and we'll provide you with a trainer who will help prepare you for team workouts in the run-up to the NBA draft. Those auditions can make a difference of millions of dollars to the players. It was a smart idea for Wasserman, and a smart investment. Believe me, I wasn't all that expensive.

I started out thinking I would try to be a college or NBA coach, but the more I got down the road of being a trainer, the more I liked it—and the more it became a viable way to make a living. Those sessions with the Wasserman guys were a huge learning experience for me, too. They gave me three of my best clients, as well as three of my best friends.

Over the years, various cities have organically evolved to be gathering places for NBA players over the summer. For a while, Chicago was the place to be. That's where Michael Jordan's longtime trainer, Tim Grover, set up shop. Las Vegas later became a popular destination, especially after the opening of the IMPACT training center, where I worked before getting hired by Wasserman. Miami had a run when LeBron James and Dwyane Wade were there, but Miami is real hot during the summer. New York is New York, but it's hard to get a gym when you need one. Space is at a premium.

Right about the time I started working with Derrick, Kevin, and Russell, Los Angeles was becoming for NBA players the place to be during the summer. In fact, I might argue that the Wasserman workouts, and those three guys in particular, were a big reason. I mean, why not L.A.? The weather is great in the summer (sunny but not too humid). You've got the beach, the bars, the restaurants, the night scene, show-biz types, all kinds of celebrities. And if Vegas is your thing, it's an easy trip. Other agencies followed Wasserman's lead in hiring their own trainers, and since many are also based in L.A., that brought even more players to town. Pickup games would take place at UCLA, Loyola Marymount, and other spots around the city. When word spread that there were intense workouts happening at this little private high school in Santa Monica, lots of other NBA guys wanted to participate.

For the most part, Russell, Derrick, and Kevin were okay with having outsiders join us. But they were picky. If somebody didn't measure up, Russ would pull me aside and say, "He ain't in our group anymore."

They took a lot of pride in their work—maybe *too* much pride. I literally had to beg those guys to take days off. I'd specifically ask them not to work out on Sunday, in hopes that it would make them fresh and ready to go when we resumed our work on Monday morning. Most of the time, they'd ignore me. I remember one time on a Sunday a buddy of mine called me from UCLA and said, "Russ is up here with his dad shooting." He always found a way to get into a gym.

Eventually I told them, "Okay, let's meet on Sunday and we'll just do some light shooting." So Sunday came, the four of us were in there alone, and we started some light shooting. It didn't take long, though, for things to get a lot less light. Russ would do a shot fake, hard dribble, elevation, and slam dunk, so Derrick and Kevin had to outdo him. Before long I was jumping right in, guarding and bumping them and talking trash. The sessions were productive, but not because my drills were so innovative. It was because of the attitude we brought to the exercise.

And then when the net work was over, the four of us would often hang out together . . . in the gym. We might be there for a while just shooting the breeze, or maybe a game of HORSE would break out. You'd think after working so hard these guys would want to get out of there, but they just loved being in the gym. It was their happy place—and mine. This was supposed to be the hard part of their job, but they never looked at it that way. It was a great lesson for me, and I continue to apply it to all my net work. The great ones find joy in the grind.

×   ×   ×

I laugh when I hear a player say, "Oh, I'm a gym rat. I'm in there working hard all day." I say if you're in the gym all day, you can't be working that hard. Do one hour with me, and I promise you'll be dead on your feet.

That's how I approach my net work: Be efficient, go hard, and then get out of here. Much of the work I put in with players takes place in the off-season. Since they have a lot more time on their hands, it's especially important to use it wisely. An NBA season is really, really long. I want them to enjoy their summers. I don't know if I've ever done double sessions with my clients, especially in July and August. They'd never make it, and it wouldn't be good for their overall development.

My whole thing is, "Don't get reps. Get *perfect* reps." If we just did something in a drill, I'm always asking, would that work in a game? If you're not going at full speed, then we're all wasting our time. Most of my workouts are no more than an hour. They're efficient, and they're high intensity. You won't see me out there talking the whole time and stopping to huddle everyone up. It's simple math: If you're not going full speed 50 reps in a workout, and you do five workouts a week, then you just wasted 250 reps. In a month it's more than 1,000.

It's amusing the response I get when I first tell an NBA player I only want him for an hour. *Really? An hour? I usually go for two or three.* Then after forty-five minutes, he's toast. "You sure you don't want to do another two hours?" I'll chide.

The details are important, but the work isn't complicated. I don't have a bunch of special secrets. That's why I bristle a bit when people call me a "shot doctor." I don't know if they're giving me too much credit or short-changing me, but that's not really what I do. I spend a lot of time, for example, helping my guys become better shooters, but I can't say I've read a lot of books or watched a lot of video to learn about technique. The main thing about teaching players to be better shooters is to make sure they practice shooting when they're *tired.* And every single shot should simulate what happens in a game. Unless we're really focusing on a guy's form, you won't find me having him stand in one place and feeding him catch-and-shoot jumpers over and over again. I'd rather they shoot a few in the corner, run across the court, catch and shoot from there, do a few more game reps, sprint down to the other end of the court, then come back and shoot again. Do that a few times, and they're gasping for air—just like in the fourth quarter. I'll never be able to replicate exactly how fatigued they are during games, but if I can't get close, then I'm not doing my job.

Personally, I think there's too much emphasis on form when it comes to shooting. Look at Tayshaun Prince. His elbow was all the way out. It was not a good-looking shot but he made threes all the time. Heck, Reggie Miller's follow-through was highly unconventional. His wrists would hit each other. I think he managed pretty well. I realize that in some cases a guy needs a fix, but almost any type of shooting technique can be grooved if the guy puts in his net work and gets enough perfect reps.

You're also not going to see me out there having my guys dribble with a bunch of tennis balls. I'm not knocking trainers who use that stuff—if it works for them and their clients, great—but my feeling is, if you're not going to use tennis balls in an NBA game, I don't want them in my workouts.

I don't go into the gym and say, "We're gonna shoot a thousand shots today." I just let it happen. And I don't want to do the same stuff every day or it becomes boring. I'm always wondering, are my guys having fun? Am I keeping them on edge, interested, and engaged? 'Cause if I'm not, they're not gonna want to spend a week with me, much less an entire summer, or several years in a row. So it's my job to come up with creative stuff, so long as it's stuff they would use in a game.

While the drills have to be changing constantly, my own energy has to be consistent—consistently *up*. The guys I'm working with are *intense*. They don't know how to be any other way, and they expect the same from me. The problem is, for them, this might be their only workout of the day. But I have to do six or seven, five or six days a week. So while I'm teaching them about basketball, they're teaching me about effort and energy. This is something important I learned early on. Effort is a talent.

Russell Westbrook exemplifies that idea better than anyone. I first met Russ at Saint Monica's the summer before his sophomore year at UCLA. He came with Kevin Love, who was about to start as a freshman. They were roommates on the road. At that point I barely knew who Russ was. He'd only played about eight minutes a game during his freshman season. Right away I thought to myself, *This guy's just a stupid athlete.* He made lots of shots, too . . . as long as they were within fifteen feet. Once he got past that mark, his shot got real flat.

That was a bad habit. I knew that was something he could improve on, but given how long that takes, I didn't want to try to fix anything so close to the season. I was worried he would get back to UCLA and his coaches would say, "Who the hell told you to do this?"

Once Russ decided to enter the NBA draft following his sophomore season, I started working with him over the course of entire summers. It was a slow process, but I could see his confidence grow week by week. You'd think his energy would decrease over time, but the opposite happened. I could pit Russ against any player, and he'd go at the guy with high intensity. Big man, point guard, swing man—it didn't matter. I was amazed at his range and his versatility.

Russ frustrates a lot of purists because he's what is known as a "volume shooter." He won't win any three-point contests or finish in the top ten in the league in that category, but he will always keep firing. What people need to understand is that this is who Russ is, and it's exactly what makes him great. He can miss twenty in a row, but he's still going to keep coming at you. Great players talk about the importance of having amnesia. That should be true if you make twenty in a row, too. Russell is a great player because he's superaggressive all the time. He's one of the best pure athletes ever to play the game. He wins like that, and loses like that. If he were to stop shooting because he missed a bunch in a row, then it would affect the rest of his game as well.

Russ is one of those guys who lives for the big moments. Some guys are wired that way. And some are wired for the opposite, by the way. We've all seen plenty of players who are really good the first three-and-a-half quarters, but when it's crunch time they suddenly become willing passers.

Russ just doesn't care what anyone thinks. Even in workouts, he has that same mentality. He can miss fifteen shots in a row and you'd never know it. He's very stone faced.

This mentality is especially crucial in the playoffs. Once you get to that point in the season, there are no secrets, and no tricks. You get into a seven-game series and after game one, the coaches don't have any more adjustments to make. Everybody knows what everybody is going to do. Scouting reports are useless. It becomes a battle of wills. Tell me who in the NBA has more sheer will than Russell Westbrook.

×   ×   ×

If a group workout is losing steam, the easiest way to revive it is by setting up a competition. It can be real simple stuff. *Let's do one-dribble pull-ups. First guy to ten wins.* Boom, it's on. The other thing I'll do to liven things up is get out there and guard guys. Of course they're a lot better than me, but they love the competition, especially when I start talking trash to them. These guys are my friends, and I know how to get in their heads.

I always end with my toughest sequence, whether it's a five-alley-oop drill or something that's high intensity. The way I look at it, you should finish the workout way harder than when you started. Same thing with bringing your best at the end of a fourth quarter. I'm trying to prepare them to not just physically but mentally play their hardest when they're at their most fatigued. There's a minute left in the game, it's the playoffs, the game is close, you have the ball . . . you have to be at your best in the moments when you feel the worst. That's how basketball—that's how life—is played.

×   ×   ×

I wasn't a great player by any stretch, but my whole life all I've done is eat, sleep, and breathe basketball. NBA, college, high school, whatever—from the time I was a kid I was obsessed with it.

You might think that because I wasn't a high-level performer that NBA players are skeptical about working with me, but that has rarely been the case. These guys are professionals, and they know that I am as well. The trust has to be there from the very beginning. It's my job as their trainer to give them confidence that I know what I'm doing.

This life—this job—is not something I planned. I just had a passion and followed it, same as the players. Net work starts with a foundation built on the idea that the only way to get somewhere is to work at your craft. From the very beginning, I understood that the key to success in basketball was the willingness to put in the time and effort. This book tells the story of that journey—what I did, where I was, and what I learned from the great ones along the way.

CHAPTER TWO

INTO THE WOODS

The court was literally surrounded by woods. It sat at the end of a path that led from an elementary school a couple of miles from the house where I grew up. Since my own driveway was too steep to play basketball on, that court in the woods was the place where I loved to play and learned to get better. It was the summer of 1998, I was twenty years old, and I had a *lot* of net work to do.

I'd been a pretty good high school player, but I didn't have a single scholarship offer from a Division I school. Not that I expected one. I was thinking I wanted to be a basketball coach, so instead of going to a Division II school to play I decided to go to Syracuse and try to walk onto the team as a nonscholarship player.

When I got to school and told people my idea, they laughed at me. I heard that most of the kids who walked onto the team made it because their families gave money to the school. I doubt that was true, but it was definitely discouraging. Still, I was pretty determined. If I was going to be a college basketball coach, what better start could I get than playing for Jim Boeheim?

During my first week on campus, I went over to the basketball offices and asked the assistant coaches if I could work out with the team. They kind of shrugged, said it was okay for me to play some pickup and do sessions with the strength coach, but that I shouldn't read that to mean I could walk onto the team. I did that for a couple of months. The team held tryouts later that fall and I thought I played pretty well. When it was over, we were told that they weren't taking any players that season.

I went to the assistants and asked them what I needed to do to make the team the following year. The consensus was that I needed to get a lot stronger. At the time I was five-eleven and 160 pounds. That wasn't going to cut it. So the rest of that school year and all through the summer I worked like a demon. Once I was back home in Rhode Island, I continued to hit the weights harder than I ever had, but mostly I spent time net working on that court in the woods. I was almost manic about it. My buddies were out partying, chasing girls, and having a great time, but I didn't drink or go out at night. All I thought about was making that team.

I didn't have a trainer, I didn't have a rebounder, and I didn't know what I was supposed to be doing. But I'd gone through this process before my senior year in high school, and I instinctively realized that I needed to go as hard as I could for as long as I could and practice shots I'd need to make in games. Combine that with all my weight lifting and I put on nearly thirty pounds of muscle.

My focus persisted after I returned to Syracuse as a sophomore. I joined a fraternity because that's what a lot of my friends did, but I told them from the beginning I wasn't doing any of that pledging crap. The coaches were impressed at how different I looked, and they said I could continue to train with the team. Once again, however, they cautioned that they couldn't make any promises.

I gotta say, the strength coach, Corey Parker, loved me. I went to all the 6:00 a.m. runs followed by hard-core weight lifting. I got to be real cool with players like Jason Hart, Tony Bland, Preston Shumpert, and Ryan Blackwell. They were way better than I was, of course, but they respected the time I was putting in.

I wish I could explain why a college sophomore with limited talent would be so intense about this. I'm not sure I understand it myself. The simplest answer is that I had a goal and truly understood what it took to get there. Nothing could distract me. I remember one night as part of the fraternity thing, these girls knocked on my door at two in the morning and wanted to party. I liked girls as much as anyone, but I knew they'd want me to chug and do all that stupid stuff, and I had absolutely no interest. Besides, I needed my sleep. I told the frat guys that if that ever happened again, I was done.

Yes, I was aware that my buddies were having more "fun" than I was, but I never experienced what kids today call FOMO—fear of missing out. I knew the odds were long, but I just wanted to give myself the maximum chance. The last thing I wanted was to get cut from the team and have to go through a bunch of what-ifs in my head.

By the time tryouts came along, I knew the guys on the team pretty well. I had a great, great tryout. I made just about everything and felt like I could hang physically. When it was over one of the assistant coaches told the group that there were no spots available, but before I could feel too disappointed he pulled me aside and told me they were keeping me.

It's hard to put into words how thrilled I was. The fact that I'd put in so many hours made it all the more gratifying.

I learned an important lesson: The harder you work, the better you feel when it pays off.

My mom told me she wanted to come up to Syracuse and take me out for a celebration dinner. I told her she didn't have to, but she's stubborn like me. My dad was in San Francisco and she didn't want to drive by herself in the winter, so she took a bus. It was twenty hours round trip, but she got there and we had our dinner. It was a night I'll never forget.

×   ×   ×

I was born and raised in Cranston, Rhode Island. I have one sister, Shana, who is eleven months older than I am to the day. We're what you call Irish twins.

My mom was a nun for seven years, but she left the convent because she wanted a family. She became a librarian at an elementary school in Providence and stayed there for thirty years. My dad became the director of the health department in Rhode Island. He was a very, very stern guy. Although they got divorced when I was eighteen, they were both very much a part of my life.

We went to church every week, but I wouldn't say it was an overly religious household. I was raised to work hard, treat elders with respect, say my prayers every night, and do well in school (or at least well enough). Then I could play and watch sports to my heart's content.

In that sense, Rhode Island was a great place to grow up. It's a small, parochial state. Everyone seems to know one another. Everyone has their little cluster of restaurants they rotate through. I think that's where I got my social nature, and why today I so aggressively build up and maintain my web of contacts. My buddies bust my chops when I take them to a game because I seem to know everyone in the arena. I wouldn't be where I am today without that skill.

I loved to play and watch every possible sport growing up, but the biggest thing for us was Providence College basketball. We had five courtside season tickets for the Friars' home games. That's when the Big East was in its heyday. I was eight years old when Rick Pitino took a team led by Billy Donovan and Delray Brooks to the 1987 Final Four. Syracuse came in with Rony Seikaly and Sherman Douglas. Georgetown had Alonzo Mourning, UConn had Ray Allen, St. John's had Ron Artest. My dad's family wanted to go to the games, too, so my sister and I would argue over who got the one spare ticket. The Big East was a league for strength and toughness. And I, literally, had a front-row seat.

That show-your-mettle mentality fit the neighborhoods where I hung out. Providence is very much a blue-collar, beer-and-shot kind of town. A big part of it is the winters. You have to be tough to get through those. There were a lot of Irish and Italian families around us, so you always felt that ethnic pride.

I mentioned how our driveway was too steep to play basketball there. Well, one day when I was about ten years old, my dad surprised me by setting up a basket on our front lawn. The rim hung over the street, so that's where we played.

Three days later, someone from the parks department came by and said we had to take the hoop down. The guy tried to argue that it wasn't safe for the boys to be on the street. My dad told him, "He's my son. Let me worry about him getting hit by a car." Then the guy gave us the real reason. Apparently our neighbors, the Mancinis, complained, and without their permission we weren't allowed to have it. So my dad took the basket down and left the pole up as a big middle finger.

It was not a cool move, but the Mancinis did me a favor because it forced me to find another place to play. That's when I started hanging around that court in the woods. When I was thirteen, I started joining the pickup games that the men in town played on the weekends. They were a lot bigger and older than I was, but I guess I eventually annoyed them enough that they had to let me play.

I *loved* that court. During the times when I might get mad at something like a typical teenager, my answer was usually to go back there and work up a sweat. It was my happy place. That's the great thing about basketball. You can do it by yourself if you want to.

When I got old enough for high school, my parents sent me to an all-boys Catholic school named Bishop Hendricken. It was a very good school with an excellent basketball program. I played for the freshman team my first year and the jayvee as a sophomore before moving up to the varsity. The team went around .500 that season but I barely got off the bench. It was tough having such a limited role on a mediocre team.

My coach, Steve Ceseretti, was an old-school guy who told you what he thought and didn't put up with any nonsense. At the end of the year he challenged me. The main thing, he said, was that I needed to be in much better shape, and I needed to improve in all areas of the game. He made it clear that if that didn't happen, I'd ride the pine again as a senior.

My limited talent was a major challenge—and in retrospect, a major blessing, because I had to learn to work hard for everything I got. I can't say I had a grand plan. I did a lot of running that summer, but mostly I did my net work on that court in the woods. Sometimes I might have a teammate come with me, but a lot of my friends worked or traveled during the summer, and since I was at a private school my friends lived all over the place. Sometimes my best friend, Brett Sylvia, would join me, but the rest of the time it was just me. The shooting drills were harder because I didn't have a rebounder, and while that seemed like a problem at the time, it actually made the workouts more helpful. I had to run after every ball myself, and I was determined to do it full speed. So I was exhausted all the time. As a result, I couldn't go that long—maybe an hour at most. I instinctively understood that net work wasn't just about form and reps. It was about simulating what it felt like to play a game.

Besides coming back to school for my senior year stronger and more skilled, I was also more confident. I knew I'd busted my butt all summer. When I stepped on the court I assumed, correctly or not, that nobody on that floor had worked as hard as I did.

The team had a terrific senior year, and so did I. I mean, my coach literally never took me out of the games. I'd hear the horn, look over at the table, assume I'd be coming out, and someone else would get subbed. We went undefeated and won the state championship in the same arena where I watched all those Providence games. It was a thrilling experience but also an important lesson, one that the great players continue to teach me to this day. If you want the glory, you better learn how to grind.

*　　*　　*

Having finally made the squad at Syracuse as a walk-on, I asked for jersey number 31, which is what I wore in high school. Nobody thought about it—I was just a walk-on, after all—but about halfway through that season it was politely pointed out to me that that number belonged to Pearl Washington, whose jersey had been retired. You can guess where I stood in that pecking order.

That said, I more than held my own during practices. I could tell after a couple of weeks that Coach Boeheim liked me because he worked me in with the scholarship guys. I'll never forget the trip the team took to Rutgers for the first Big East game of the season. The coaches usually brought each walk-on to two road trips per year. The team was headed out after practice. When it was over, I showered and was getting ready to go home when Boeheim saw me. "Where are you going?" he asked.

"Back to my room," I replied. I told him how the walk-ons could only go to two games per year.

Boeheim turned to an assistant and said, "Rob is coming to every game with us."

Fine by me, Coach.

As you can imagine, I almost never got into the actual games. The official record shows that I played six games and made one field goal during my sophomore season, and played in eight games with two buckets as a junior. I was getting basically the same scrub duty at the start of my senior year, but I started off by hitting my first three three-pointers. One came late in a blowout win over Colgate. The shot clock was off and the game was winding down, but I let it fly anyway. Man, was Boeheim pissed. One of the assistants, Mike Hopkins, came up to me afterward to ask what the hell I was thinking. "What's he gonna do, not play me?" I said.

The next day, Hop walked into practice and showed me a printout of the national stats rankings on ESPN.com. I was ranked first in the country in three-point percentage. He made a bunch of copies and taped one in everyone's locker. As you can imagine, I got my balls busted pretty good that day. The next time I got into a game, I had a chance to shoot a wide-open three, but I pump faked and drove it because I didn't want to ruin my perfect record.

Later that season, Boeheim put me into a competitive game for the first time. It happened late in the first half against Seton Hall. One of our guards had just picked up his third foul, and Boeheim looked down the bench and said, "Rob, get in there." I froze in my seat. Hop had to shout at me to snap me out of it. Next thing I knew, I was guarding Seton Hall point guard Shaheen Holloway. I did my best for a few minutes, and then there was a time-out. I thought Boeheim would sub for me, but he left me in until halftime. I can't say I really helped, but at least I didn't screw up too badly.

I didn't care that I wasn't playing in the games. I was having too much fun. My last two years in college, I got to spend a week during the summer working at Michael Jordan's camp for kids in Chicago. The counselors there included some pretty good college players—guys like Darius Miles, Drew Gooden, and Juan Dixon. During my first year there, Michael's son Marcus was on a team I was coaching. I didn't play Marcus at all in the first game, but during the second one Michael walked over and sat behind our bench. I immediately sent Marcus into the game. Then I heard a familiar, deep voice behind me. "Do what you gotta do, man," Michael said. "Don't worry about me."

The best part of those weeks was the evening pickup games with the counselors. That gave me a chance to play against some really good college players. And on one memorable evening, it gave me a chance to play against arguably the greatest player ever.

I remember it was real late, around ten o'clock at night. We were finishing up a game and Michael walked into the gym with a cigar. We were pretty dead, having played for several hours, but when Michael shouted "I got next!" you can bet we perked up. We stuck around for a while longer, and during one game I got to be on his team.

Michael would jump into some of our games during the week. During one game, he was on the opposite team, and we were all looking at one another like, Who's going to guard this guy? No problem. I stepped in, checked the ball to the great MJ, and got in my defensive stance. He smiled at me and said, "There's not one white guy in the NBA who can guard me. Why would you think you can do it?"

I'm thinking, *This isn't real.* First time he leans like he's driving to his left, and as soon as I try to cut him off, he switches over to his right and lays it in at the rim. On the next possession, I got the ball deep on the wing. I guess Michael didn't take me that seriously—I mean, why would he?—so I let it fly. Swish! Damn straight I let him know about it. He pretty much dominated me the rest of the way, but it was still the thrill of a lifetime. Best of all, after the game one of the managers came up to me and said he had the whole thing on videotape. I still have it as proof that it really happened.

✳   ✳   ✳

Don't get me wrong, I did have a social life at Syracuse. That end of things got much better once people realized I was on the team. But everything revolved around the team. The players were a very close-knit group. We went to dinner and parties together. We were really a family.

It wasn't just the time we spent together, it was the sacrifices. We didn't get breaks over Thanksgiving or Christmas. We usually had a game on December 27, which meant we'd practice on Christmas night. I remember being a little depressed when I left my house in Rhode Island on Christmas morning to climb into my red station wagon and make the six-hour drive back to school. Winters are pretty miserable in Syracuse and there's not much to do there anyway. So I ended up spending almost all my time with my teammates. To this day many are my closest friends.

Yes, I was still a walk-on (I never had the gumption to ask Boeheim to put me on scholarship), but I was a senior now and had been there long enough to talk trash to everyone. But the really cool thing that happened that year is how I started to get closer to Coach Boeheim. The guy was such a legend and I was always afraid to approach him, but I discovered that he was very easy to talk to. First of all, he's a sports nut, just like me. We'd talk about all kinds of sports as well as what was going on with our own team. Those conversations are some of my fondest memories from college.

Since I knew I wanted to be a coach, I paid close attention to how Coach Boeheim went about his job. The first thing that came through was his intensity. When practice begins everyone in the gym knows who's in charge. He delegates most of the player development stuff to his assistants, which allows him to devote all of his mental and physical energy to practice. When drills are going on, Boeheim doesn't miss a thing. He is constantly raising everyone's standards.

Boeheim's practices were competitive but rarely long. They didn't go for three hours. They were closer to an hour and a half. We played zone defense all the time so there wasn't a lot of scouting to do. That's one of the many reasons Boeheim loves playing the zone. It means there's less information he has to pass along to the players. He likes to stick to the basics.

The most impressive thing about Boeheim is how strong he is as a game coach. First, he's usually very calm. I see all these coaches screaming and sweating and stomping their feet, and I know that only makes their players more nervous. Boeheim isn't like that. He doesn't mind if you miss a few shots. He wants you to keep playing and believing the next one is going to go in.

Boeheim is a very smart, analytical guy. He's always reading, mostly mystery novels. He likes solving puzzles. That's why the zone is so perfect for him. He can tweak it any way he wants to account for what the other team is doing. I've seen him make one or two minor adjustments at halftime, and in the second half we'd be a completely different team.

By watching Boeheim teach the zone, I learned the value of simplicity. That's what really makes the defense work. I remember picking his brain about it, because I was having a hard time understanding why offenses so consistently had trouble figuring the thing out. Boeheim pointed out to me that when coaches play a zone, if the other team makes a couple of buckets, they immediately switch to man-to-man. "I play percentages," he said. "If they make a few outside shots, I figure they won't be able to keep it up. I'm actually more worried when they miss outside shots because it means they'll try to go inside."

Maybe my biggest takeaway from being around Boeheim for three years was the calmness he showed when games got tense. He can be tough on his guys in practice, but when the game comes around, he wants them to be loose, so he lets them play. Not only does he not give his players a lot of information in scouting reports, he's one of the few coaches who doesn't do game-day shootarounds. He'd rather they rest and keep their minds clear.

This is the approach I try to take with my workouts. I don't need to yell at my guys—and it's not because, technically, I work for them. I don't freak out if they have a bad workout or miss a bunch of shots. I want them to stay calm, remain confident, and trust their instincts. And by the way, the same holds true if they make a bunch of shots in a row. We don't need to be going nuts and raising the roof out there. We're there to work. Just like Boeheim, I try to keep things on an even keel.

My college years gave me my first close-up view of how big-time players go about their business. Nobody worked harder than Jason Hart, a six-foot-three guard from Los Angeles. Jason and I became fast friends, largely because he was one of the few dudes who was even crazier than I was when it came to net work. He would do a full-scale workout with Hopkins for an hour or two before practice, then stay an hour later after it was over. If we had a seven o'clock game, Jason and Hop would get their net work in around 4:00 p.m. If Jason had a bad game, win or lose, he and Hop would be back in the Dome to work out late that night.

Jason wasn't a naturally gifted shooter. He really had to work at it. He may not have been the most talented player ever to come through Syracuse, but that approach and focus helped him play ten years in the NBA.

I was mesmerized by those workouts, not just because of how hard Jason worked, but because of how hard Hop worked as well. That guy was a fire hose of energy. He wasn't just rebounding and feeding Jason passes. He was guarding him, taking charges, moving with him, talking trash. If he stopped Jason's forward progress or messed with his shot, he'd yell at him, "You're nothing!" It helped make the sessions fun as well as competitive. It made me realize that player development isn't just about skills and footwork. It's about attitude, approach, intensity, purpose, efficiency—all those things. Teaching skills was actually the easy part.

When Hop played for Syracuse, he was known as the first guy to dive on the floor and get blood on his face. He knew he wasn't going to come in and score thirty points a game. His ticket to minutes was showing effort, sacrifice, smarts, and toughness. Hop was great with Jason, but the truth is he was like that with *all* the guys. If you wanted to work out, he never turned you down, no matter what time it was. He was totally dedicated.

I hope my clients think the same of me. It's a big reason why I don't have a staff under me. One of my big pitches to players is, "If you hire me, you get *me*." I want to be available and dedicated to them the same way Hop was to the guys at Syracuse. I know he's the same way these days as the head coach at the University of Washington.

✻   ✻   ✻

I finally took another three-pointer in the closing minute of our NCAA tournament loss to Kansas. My playing career (such as it was) ended that night. In many ways, my experience as a walk-on at Syracuse set me up for the rest of my life. I learned a lot and formed friendships that sustain me to this day.

I'm still friends with Coach Boeheim, too, but it's different. When you meet someone at that point in your life and you look up to him, you never really get past it. Coach Boeheim isn't someone who'll tell you how much he likes you or how proud he is of you, but he has ways of letting you know. During the summer of 2012, he was an assistant with the Team USA squad that played in the London Olympics. Several of my clients were on the team, so I was in Las Vegas for the week helping them out.

One day Coach Boeheim invited me out to dinner with the staff. When I got there, he introduced me to all the coaches and bragged to them how I used to be his walk-on and now I train all the biggest NBA stars. He wouldn't tell me directly how proud he was, so it was gratifying to hear him say it to other people. That night I sat at dinner between Coach Boeheim and Mike Krzyzewski and all the USA Basketball royalty. If you didn't know better, you'd have thought I belonged.

The next day, after one of the USA practices, I went onto the court and did a quick session with Kevin Durant, Kevin Love, and Derrick Rose. At one point I looked over and saw Coach Boeheim sitting on the side, watching us do our net work. It was a full-circle moment.

CHAPTER THREE

FROM PE TO KG

Jim Boeheim knew I wanted to be a college coach, and he'd offered to help me any way he could. After my senior season was over, he put in a good word for me with Seth Greenberg, the head coach at South Florida. I was hired sight unseen as a graduate assistant. I borrowed a little cash from my ninety-five-year-old grandmother, drove down there in my mom's car, and went to work on a whopping $10,000 salary.

One of my responsibilities was to help prepare scouting reports of opponents. You'd think my insights would be helpful when we played at Syracuse in the ninth game, but we lost anyway, 80–68. That was definitely a little weird for me, sitting on the visitors' bench in the Carrier Dome.

As a South Florida graduate assistant (no faculty position involved; I was just taking classes), I wasn't on the road recruiting, but once in a while I'd ride with the other assistants to check out players around the state. One of the high schools we visited often was IMG Academy, a private school in Bradenton. There, I'd see guys who were brought in to drill players in skills and conditioning. This was the first time it dawned on me that people could do player development as a full-time career. Since that was the aspect of coaching that interested me the most, I asked the coaches at South Florida if I could work out some of our guys. I was young and single, which meant I was always available. The players were into it, and I channeled my inner Mike Hopkins in an attempt to make them better.

When the school year was over, I drove straight back to Rhode Island without stopping. I just wanted to get home and figure out what the heck I was going to do with my life. I had no money and no prospects, so I moved in with my mother. Since the only thing I knew was basketball, I decided to make a few bucks training aspiring players. Of course, there was no social media back then. I had to use regular, old-fashioned shoe leather to get the word out. I hung up flyers around town and put my name in church bulletins.

Fortunately, a lot of well-off families came up to Rhode Island to vacation during the summer. A friend of mine connected me to one, and I was soon training a twelve-year-old boy and his fourteen-year-old sister on an outdoor court on a hot summer day. It was my first official gig.

How, you might ask, did I know what to do? Well, I did and I didn't. It's not like I studied a ton of videos and books to come up with drills and concepts. I was never one of those guys who constantly scribbled in notebooks. Mostly, I went by instinct. I was a lifelong basketball junkie, and I'd spent all those hours watching the Syracuse coaches work out me and the other players. I'd put myself through all those rigorous sessions on that court in the woods. Everything I'd seen taught me that workouts should be short, efficient, and intense. The rest was just details.

After the session was over, the mom approached me and asked how much I charged. I wasn't sure what the going rate was, so I said, "Forty bucks."

"Are you kidding me?" she asked.

I thought I'd overpriced myself, so I told her I would take thirty. She shook me off again. "I'm not giving you less than eighty," she said. "If you did that on Long Island, you'd get one fifty."

One fifty? Hey, I might be onto something here.

It ended up being a pretty good summer. I found a few other families who wanted me to work out their kids. I'd charge fifty bucks an hour for a kid, or eighty for two kids. If I could get a bigger group together that meant more money for me and less money from each family. I picked up clients purely through word of mouth.

I can honestly say that having local teenagers as clients instead of Division I players didn't cause me to approach the training more casually. To me, basketball is basketball. If you're my client and you love the game as much as I do, we're going to go hard. There's no short-changing anyone when it comes to net work.

*   *   *

The best thing that came out of all those trips to IMG Academy was that it allowed me to meet Joe Abunassar, the school's director of basketball. He was well known in the sport because he trained some of the NBA's biggest names, including Kevin Garnett, Chauncey Billups, Tayshaun Prince, Al Harrington, and Tyronn Lue.

After I returned to Rhode Island, I called Joe and asked if I could intern at one of his summer camps. He warned me it didn't pay well but said okay. I made the long drive to Florida, and for a month I did whatever he asked. While I worked with the kids, Joe trained the pros. Vince Carter came there for a week and was amazing. Those were some long, hot days. IMG didn't have its own gym back then, so we had to bus the kids to local facilities, some of which weren't even air-conditioned.

All this time I was looking for a college job (because South Florida had just been a one-year thing), but came up empty. When September rolled around, I was still unemployed. So I went to my old high school, Bishop Hendricken, and asked the principal, Vin Mancuso, who was a basketball assistant coach when I was there, if there were any jobs I could fill. As it turned out, he'd recently lost a phys ed teacher. Because it's a private school, a master's degree wasn't necessary to teach there—and it's not like an advanced education is required to teach dodgeball anyway. So I told Vin I was interested, and I asked the head basketball coach, Jamal Gomes, if I could be an assistant on the varsity. He said he'd love to have me.

The job paid all of $26,500 with benefits, but I was an ambitious guy. After my day was over at two-thirty, I continued to do paid workouts on the side. The school was great about allowing me to use the gym. Word was really getting out about me, and it helped that I was working with one of the top basketball programs in the state.

We had a couple of promising freshman guards on the team in Joe Mazzula and Jimmy Baron. Jimmy's father, Jim Sr., was the head coach at the University of Rhode Island. Those guys were absolute gym rats. I'd meet them at six every morning to work them out. I never charged them; I just loved doing it. During their last two years at the school, we won the state title. Both of those guys became very good college players. Joe started for the West Virginia team that made the 2010 Final Four, and Jimmy played for his dad at URI and left school as the Atlantic 10's all-time leading three-point shooter.

I hoarded my sick days so I could go to the Final Four that spring and continue looking for a college coaching job. When nothing came of that, I was stuck going into yet another summer without a full-time gig. I called Joe again and asked if I could work IMG's summer camp, but my real goal was to find a spot at the prestigious ABCD Camp in Teaneck, New Jersey. That was the camp run by the godfather of summer hoops, Sonny Vaccaro. He used to work for Nike, but after Nike fired him he took his brand and breadth of contacts over to Adidas. Sonny always got the top high school players to go to ABCD. Besides the chance to work with those kids, the camp would offer me a chance to press the flesh with people around college hoops.

I asked everyone I knew to put in a good word for me with Sonny, but I couldn't get hold of him. A friend of mine named Bobby Hartstein, who was the coach at Lincoln High School in Brooklyn, gave me Sonny's fax number and suggested I send him my résumé. So I did. No response. Next day, same thing. No response. I kept this up every day for three weeks—no joke. Finally Bobby called me and told me I had a spot in the camp.

On the first day, I introduced myself to Sonny and thanked him for letting me in. "I didn't have a choice!" he said. "You were relentless! My wife would have killed me if I didn't invite you."

That week was the first time I can remember feeling genuinely overwhelmed. There were more than two hundred kids at the camp, dozens of coaches teaching them, and several thousand college coaches in the bleachers watching all the action. I got paired with Matt Doherty, who'd just been let go as the head coach at North Carolina. Our team had three high school All Americans who would all end up playing in the NBA—Andray Blatche, O. J. Mayo, and Bill Walker. Basically, though, I was everybody's gopher that week.

Not surprisingly, I was most interested in the group workouts that took place in the morning. Most of those were run by Tim Grgurich, a basketball lifer who was the head coach at the University of Pittsburgh for a few years and has worked as an NBA assistant for several teams. Grgurich has mentored a lot of coaches, including Mike Hopkins, so it was extremely valuable to see him in action. I could see where Mike got his ideas about energy and intensity. Grgurich was really in the players' faces, but it was all very positive. These were young kids, and they wouldn't have responded well to someone yelling and demeaning them.

While I was picking up work back in Rhode Island, I got connected with a player named Ruben Garces. He'd played on the Providence team that made it to the Elite Eight in 1997 and had been overseas for a number of years. This was the first time I worked consistently with a professional player. After he returned to Spain, Ruben paid for me to fly there to keep working with him. We got so close that Ruben named me as his son's godfather. This began a pattern. Players started out as clients, but quickly became my close friends.

×   ×   ×

As I was training Ruben, another player who was hanging out in the gym started asking to join us. His name was Ryan Gomes, and he was heading into his sophomore year at Providence. Ryan was six-foot-seven so he pretty much played the same position as Ruben. He was intrigued by how we were developing Ruben's skills away from the basket. I

didn't know Ryan well and he didn't have much of a reputation, but I was around the program a lot and went to
many of their games. I was happy to help him out.

Ryan wasn't one of those players who came to college
expecting the program to springboard him immediately to
the NBA. He was an undersized center who was supposed
to redshirt his freshman year. The only reason he didn't
redshirt was that the team's center got hurt eight games
into the season, and the coaches decided Ryan needed to
play. He had fifteen points and eight rebounds in his first
game. As a sophomore he averaged eighteen points and
ten rebounds.

Ryan helped me realize that, in pursuing a career as a
trainer, it wouldn't matter that I hadn't played the game at
a high level. I think he appreciated how hard I had to work
just to be a walk-on at Syracuse, and in that time we were
working together my lack of elite playing credentials became
something I stopped worrying about. I was teaching ball,
he was playing ball, and we were both trying to get better.

The first thing I noticed about Ryan was that his shot
looked pretty good. He possessed nice form and balance,
and when we were practicing he shot with confidence. Right
away I encouraged him to develop that skill. I'm not sure
anyone had ever said that to him before. I made clear to
him that if he ever got a tryout with the pros, he'd have
a hard time scoring on the block over bigger players, so
he'd better figure out how to get it done on the perimeter.
It's not like Tim Welsh, the Providence coach, was holding
him back, but Ryan was such an effective scorer inside that
at that time it would have been foolish to ask him to move
away from the basket. When the season started I'd go to
the games at Providence, and sometimes afterward we'd
get a bite to eat.

We put in a lot of time together the following summer. Donnie McGrath, who was the PC point guard at the time, joined us as well. At the time Providence had only one gym, and sometimes another team would be in there. So we'd go to Bishop Hendricken or some other gym in town. It took a few weeks but soon Ryan was making real progress as a shooter. The more shots dropped through the net, the more he wanted to work at it.

A big key for Ryan was getting down his footwork. We did some drills where he had to dribble the ball between his legs, step back, and fire. It was a lot to get used to. I was far more interested in the fundamentals of the move than whether the ball actually went in. I knew that would come in time. The main thing was that Ryan had to develop those lower-body skills, because one consequence of his eventually becoming a small forward was that he'd have to guard smaller players. It was a major shift for him.

Ryan also made a major shift in his thinking. He really hadn't considered himself an NBA player, or even given much thought to the notion that he could make money playing overseas. Once he realized that was a realistic goal, he locked in. It helped that he worked with Ruben, because even though Ruben wasn't in the NBA, he was making a healthy income overseas. And going up against Ruben every day made Ryan a lot better. It was easy to motivate Ryan once that became his focus. When he'd get tired, I could say to him, "You can rest if you want, but if you want to be a pro, you gotta keep going." That put him right back on the floor.

Slowly but surely, his confidence grew. At first, if he missed a bunch of shots in a row he'd get discouraged, but later on when he had a bad stretch it wouldn't faze him as much. That's because there were fewer of those. He was such a naturally gifted shooter, it really surprised me he hadn't used it more. When his junior year began, he was ready to do just that.

I still had my family's courtside seats to Providence games, so I could monitor his progress up close. I remember one game where he missed a few in a row—he looked over at me with this perplexed look on his face. I raised up my right arm, showing that he needed to follow through better. Tim Welsh, the Friars coach, saw that exchange, and I think he was a little confused.

Ryan didn't make a single three-pointer in his first two years in college, but he made twenty-nine threes on 33 percent shooting as a junior. The following summer he came to Florida to work out with me at IMG. He'd put his name into the NBA draft and wanted to get ready for the workouts. We spent more than a month together, all with the intent of making him more effective facing up away from the basket. He did well in the workouts, but when he couldn't get a promise he'd be a first-round pick, he decided to go back to Providence for his senior year.

Ryan had a stellar final season, averaging twenty-two points and eight rebounds while shooting 38 percent from the three-point arc. He'd gone from an under-recruited redshirt candidate to an All-American. After his senior year was over, I helped him get ready for the draft. We had a good group of guys to work with—Sebastian Telfair, Chris (Birdman) Anderson, Jared Dudley, Taurean Green. We'd work out in the Tarkanian Center. At that point I had very high ambitions for Ryan as a shooter. "You should never miss two in a row," I told him. "And you definitely can't miss three. If you miss it, correct it the next shot. You're too good."

Ryan was always a soft-spoken kid. He was not one to do a lot of trash talking or be real vocal. But on the court he was a killer. He was also a really good leader, especially that senior year. It was impressive to see him grow into himself. The first time he ever played organized basketball was as a freshman in high school. He always needed other people to tell him how good he was before he believed it himself. He'd never been hyped as a big-time recruit so he felt as though he had a lot to prove. I think he surprised himself with how good he had become.

I never asked Ryan to pay me for those summer workouts when he was in college. Most of the time I was in the gym anyway, so it wasn't a burden to let him join our sessions. It actually made things better to create a small group. But though I didn't quite anticipate it at the time, my work with Ryan was teaching me a lot about how to develop players. I was still thinking about becoming a coach as opposed to a full-time trainer, but either way the knowledge was a huge boon for me at an early age. I started to understand what it took to become a professional, how long it took to develop these skills, and the importance of not setting limits. The fact that you've never used these skills before doesn't mean you won't or can't in the future. If you're willing to put in the net work, you can improve more than you realized was possible.

Ryan ended up playing seven years in the NBA with the Celtics, Timberwolves, Clippers, and Thunder. I worked with him during his first couple of years in the NBA, but we've remained good friends long after we stopped training together. Throughout his career I'd watch him closely and call or text him with my thoughts. He knew I'd seen his development from the early days, and that I'd always tell him exactly what I thought without being a jerk about it. He never felt that I was going to give him less thought or attention because I was starting to work with All-Stars. We were good friends, and that's something you just can't fake.

✳   ✳   ✳

After working as a phys ed teacher at Bishop Hendricken from 2002 to 2005, I thought I'd finally found a real job coaching big-time basketball. The Syracuse staff had hooked me up with someone who ran the junior national team in Norway. He hired me to coach their team, so I decided to head over there for the season. I also wrote to every NBA team to see if I could pick up some work on the side scouting European players.

The Pistons and the Cavaliers had expressed some interest, so I was pretty well set—or so I thought. A few days before I was supposed to leave, the guy who ran the team told me he could only pay me half of what he promised. The Syracuse coaches were emphatic that I shouldn't go. It wasn't worth it if I couldn't trust the guy I'd be working for.

The problem was, I'd already quit my job at Bishop Hendricken. It was too late to go back, so I had to really dedicate myself to finding people to work out. I also set up a few camps and clinics. Fortunately, the school still let me use the gym, but I really had to hustle for clients. My mom thought she was finally getting rid of me, but I ended up staying with her awhile longer. I busted my tail that winter and spring developing my training business, but my main aspiration was still to make it in coaching somewhere.

I was back at ABCD the following summer. This was my third stint there, and I started to really feel like I belonged. They gave me some more responsibilities working out the campers between games. It's funny because I still hadn't done any note taking or collecting special drills, but I was starting to develop my own way of doing things. I ran work-outs in a way that fit my personality. That doesn't mean my ways were better than anyone else's, but they were right for me.

That summer at ABCD I met two players whom I'd eventually become very close to, Kevin Love and Derrick Rose. We didn't spend a ton of time together, but we made a connection, and it was something we could build on. In fact, the whole concept of networking—not just net working—was really coming into focus for me.

After my week at ABCD was over, I went to Florida again to work the IMG camp. It was the same routine as always—that is, until Joe needed to fly out somewhere and asked me to work out Kevin Garnett in his absence.

I'd never worked out a single NBA player before. "Can't I start with a sixth man or something?" I joked.

"Just do what I do and you'll be fine," Joe said.

I don't think KG knew who I was. I rebounded for him a few times during Joe's workouts, but that was the extent of our interactions. I liked what Joe did, but he had a different type of personality from me. He wasn't inclined to jump into a drill, guard a guy, and talk trash. I wasn't sure if I should tone it down or be myself, so I figured I'd go on instinct.

Kevin came into the gym later that day all business-like. Joe had told him I'd be running the workout, and he seemed cool with it. I started with a simple jab step and shot from the block, after which he'd flash from side to side. Kevin got into the drill, set up on the block, made his move . . . and screamed, *"Aaaaarrrgghhhh!!"*

Whoa.

He screamed like that on the next shot as well, and the next, and every one after. Every move he made, he went hard, always letting out the same guttural *Aaaaarrrgghhhh!!* I'd never seen such intensity in my life, and it didn't take long for me to get caught up in it. I had someone else to rebound for us, so pretty quick I was jumping into the drill, guarding Kevin, yelling at him. He looked at me with an expression that said, are you serious? If he missed a couple of shots, he'd smack himself on the head and curse himself out. I thought things would die down a little once the workout got going, but it never did. I got so into it that I forgot to give him a break. After about thirty minutes he said, "Bro, can I get some water?"

I didn't try to give him anything too complicated. I wanted to stick to moves he'd use in a game. He didn't know me, and I wanted him to be comfortable, but the truth is that he's the one who made me comfortable. He just wanted to get some work in, and he trusted me to be his guide.

That's something that great players have in common. They don't walk into the gym acting like they know it all. They walk in looking to learn something new.

Over the years I've had clients who asked all sorts of questions. Why this? Why that? I'm like, really? Why are you questioning me? I'm not saying I have all the answers, but I have a job to do, and presumably so do you. Ironically, none of the truly great players I've trained have ever questioned me. They might ask me a few things just to clarify what I want, but they never show skepticism.

That afternoon at IMG was a big moment for me. It did wonders for my confidence, and it gave me a great vantage point to understand how the great ones go about their net work. It was mind boggling to see that kind of focus and intensity up close. It was an experience I'll never forget.

×   ×   ×

My coaching break still wasn't coming, but I did get presented with a terrific opportunity that fall of 2006. Joe Abunassar called to say that he was starting his own training center in Las Vegas called IMPACT. He was still going to be shuttling back and forth to IMG Academy, but he needed someone to run the Vegas business full-time. Besides the fact that I had no other good prospects, it was a no-brainer. The job paid $45,000 a year, and Vegas wasn't a real expensive place to live.

I had a serious girlfriend by then, so the two of us moved to Vegas. I worked primarily with kids' camps off the bat and also with a lot of high school teams. There were a few international high schools that would come to town and we'd have them in for a week. It was just a way to keep some money coming in until the NBA guys could spring loose for full-time training the following off-season.

As luck would have it, the 2007 NBA All-Star Game was held in Las Vegas in February. It was a crazy scene all over the city, and not necessarily in a good way. There were so many fights that the cops had to shut down Las Vegas Boulevard at times. The clubs were packed at night, and people really cut loose. That insanity aside, it was a great couple of days for IMPACT, because we were one of the few gyms that was available. Several NBA players who weren't All-Stars came to get workouts over the five-day break and be around the festivities.

A few of the players who came to our gym were represented by Arn Tellem, B. J. Armstrong, and Bob Myers, the top basketball agents at Wasserman Media Group in Los Angeles. Joe had helped work out their clients for predraft workouts. He was working at one end of the gym, and I was at the other. I was doing my usual thing—grabbing pads, jumping into the drills, sweating my ass off. I talked a little bit with the agents but didn't think much of it.

The following spring, I got a call from someone at Wasserman asking if I'd come out to L.A. to meet with their NBA agents. I didn't know what it was about, but of course I was up for it. I went out to Arn's house. It was pretty intimidating. I mean, the guy was—is—a legend. B.J. and Bob were there, and they told me that they wanted to create a "player development coach" position at their agency, someone their clients could work with as they prepared for the draft.

The agents play a big role in the whole predraft process. The first big event is the combine in Chicago. It actually used to be a much bigger deal, but nowadays the agents who represent the top players advise them all not to play. I can't say I blame them. The five-on-five games at the combine don't give players much opportunity to showcase themselves to the league. Why give the teams something to question if you have a bad game or two? The real action at the combine is the team interviews. Each team will submit a list of players it wants to meet with and will spend days in a hotel conference room getting a feel for their personalities.

After that, agents need to select which teams their clients are going to work out for, and when. If an agent reps a top player, he'll often insist that the workout not involve any other players or contact. Most players, however, don't have that kind of leverage. Still, it's a very strategic process. The goal isn't just to impress the NBA teams but also to keep from doing something that will lower your stock. There are millions of dollars at stake. It's smart to be cautious, to say the least.

Most scouts and general managers will have seen the prospects play in college multiple times, sometimes going back to high school. They have a good feel for what the players can do. The main question the teams have to answer is which players fill their needs and fit their system. Anyone can draft from the top four or five spots. Once you get deeper into the draft, those nuances make all the difference.

No agency had ever tried to hire a trainer specifically to prepare its clients for the draft the way Wasserman was proposing, but I was definitely up for it. I can't say Joe was thrilled with my leaving him so soon. I moved with my girlfriend to L.A. and found a small apartment in Playa del Rey, where we lived with our Yorkshire terrier, Clutch.

The college season had finished up so I dove right into the workouts at Saint Monica's with guys like Mike Dunleavy, Jason Kapono, J. J. Redick, and Antawn Jamison. Ryan Gomes was also there. The Wasserman agents would come and watch, but they never told me what to do. I didn't expect that—especially from B.J., who'd played in the NBA for eleven years and won three titles with the Bulls—but I sure appreciated it. It showed they trusted me.

The main thing was, I knew they wanted me to keep things simple. It's like what they say about doctors: "First, do no harm." My job was to make sure their clients were in shape so they'd perform well in their workouts with NBA teams.

That was a big spring for Wasserman because the agency ended up having seven of the top fifteen picks. That included Derrick Rose and Russell Westbrook as well as the Lopez twins (Brook and Robin), Danilo Gallinari, Anthony Randolph, and D. J. Augustin.

For most of the time I was in L.A., I was doing individual and small group sessions for our draft prospects. We kept the gym low-key—no media or scouts. Then in early June, Wasserman had a pro day where they invited representatives from all thirty NBA teams to the school to watch their clients work out. This was a big event for the players, but it was also huge for me. All the higher-ups were going to be there, including head coaches and general managers. NBA TV was there to film it. I was nervous, to say the least. There I was on the court warming up my guys, and I looked over and saw R. C. Buford, Jerry West, Magic Johnson, Pat Riley—all the big names.

I knew I'd only look good if my guys looked good. So I set up the workout to play to their strengths. Obviously, I wasn't going to have Derrick and Russell shoot a bunch of threes. D. J. Augustin, on the other hand, was a great shooter, so when it was his turn that's what I showcased. All along I was hoping this would lead to a gig as an NBA assistant. I'll never forget when Pat Riley came up to me afterward and said, "I loved what you did out there." I was in awe of that guy.

The NBA's predraft combine was in Orlando, so I went down there to be on hand in case any of the Wasserman clients wanted to get in some extra floor time. A few weeks later, I was at Arn Tellem's house in L.A. to watch the draft lottery with everyone. It came down to Miami and Chicago for the first pick. It was pretty well known that Derrick would be the top pick, so this was going to determine where he'd go. He was the ultimate Chicago kid, and the franchise was really in a bad spot (which is why they were in the lottery). When the Bulls were awarded the top pick, Derrick had this delighted, disbelieving look on his face. There'd be excitement and a whole lot of pressure, but he'd just found out that he was going to be the face of the team he'd rooted for growing up. He was going home, this time with a multimillion-dollar contract and the prestige of being the number-one pick in the NBA draft.

I joined the Wasserman guys in New York the night of the draft. When it was over, the agency threw a party for the players and their families. It ended after midnight, at which point Arn, B.J., and I found a local deli and ordered some huge sandwiches. That meal culminated not just a long night for them but several months of wheeling and dealing—signing players, arranging workouts, maneuvering so their clients would be drafted into the best situations. I was a small part of that process, more of an observer than anything, but it was my first real look inside the business of the NBA. I don't know that I felt as if I were any closer to my dream of being an NBA coach, but I did feel that I'd been invited inside a very powerful, exclusive family. Not bad for a former walk-on, right?

CHAPTER FOUR

DERRICK ROSE

It was Halloween night 2018. I was sitting in my basement man cave, with its comfortable couch, player jerseys hanging all around, and a 120-inch flat-screen on the wall. As usual, I was flipping through games on NBA League Pass and tracking my clients. I was keeping a special eye on the Minnesota Timberwolves' game against the Utah Jazz. Derrick Rose was starting for the T-Wolves that night because a few of the regular starters were injured. After many years suffering devastating injuries and bouncing around to different teams, Derrick had had a terrific summer working out with me in L.A. We were both hoping that all that net work would pay off.

Outside shooting had always been the weakest part of Derrick's game, so we spent a lot of time on that over the summer. We didn't do anything different than we'd done in summers past. The difference was, he could show up more consistently because he was finally healthy. He didn't have to take a day off two or three times a week. He could string together five or six days. He went as hard as ever.

That Halloween night, I was encouraged when Derrick hit a few shots early in the first quarter. It was great to see the ball go in, but mostly it was uplifting to see him shooting with confidence again. Even on his misses, he was firing as if he thought it was going in.

Except he wasn't missing much. He drained a few long jump shots in the first quarter. I flipped through the channels, then back, and saw him make some more shots. *Hmmm, this could be something.* I texted Derrick's agent, B. J. Armstrong, and asked if he was watching. "Oh, yeah, I'm watching," he wrote back. Remarkably, Derrick had twenty-six at the half. I figured I should stick around and watch the rest of the game.

What I saw astounded and delighted me as much as anything in my career. Derrick ended up scoring a career-high fifty points. Minnesota won, 128–125. The only thing better than seeing that ball go in so often was watching the reaction of Derrick's teammates on the bench. They were going absolutely nuts. They seemed even happier for him than he was for himself. Everyone in the NBA knew exactly what Derrick had been through. In 2011, he was voted as the youngest MVP in the history of the league, but now he was just trying to prove he belonged. No matter how bad things got for him, Derrick always treated other people well.

As soon as the game ended, Derrick's teammates surrounded him and hugged him. When he was interviewed at half-court, he got emotional. "Words can't explain what I feel right now," he said as he wiped tears from his eyes with a towel. "It's been a while."

Derrick is usually a pretty stoic guy. He doesn't show his emotions easily. Sitting on my couch at home, I got emotional, too. Derrick is one of my oldest clients and closest friends. I was one of the few people who really and truly understood what he'd been through. We texted after the game, but I waited a couple of days to call him because I knew his phone would be blowing up. "Rob Maaaack," he said, answering with his usual greeting.

"So," I said. "Fifty piece, huh?"

Derrick laughed. "I had to let 'em know, Mac! I had to let 'em know."

I loved hearing that joy in his voice. There were too many times over the years when we spoke and it wasn't there. I told Derrick that what really moved me was how many NBA players reached out to me to express how happy they were. "I hope you know how they all feel about you," I told him. Other guys like Dwyane Wade and LeBron James said similar things about him on Twitter. It was a big night for the NBA.

A few reporters called me right after Derrick's performance. They all wanted to know what magical thing we concocted over the summer to produce this new version of the former MVP. I told them all the same thing. Derrick's improvement didn't happen over the summer. It was the culmination of ten years' worth of net working.

That's why he got so emotional. He knew how long and hard his journey was to get to that moment. He'd taken a beating in the media and from the fans in his last couple of years with the Bulls and Knicks. For much of the time, he was too hurt to play, and when he did play, his body wasn't strong enough for him to be effective. Once he got healthy and strong, and once his lifelong confidence came back, D. Rose was ready to play like D. Rose again. The net work paid off.

*　　*　　*

The first time I met Derrick Rose was at the ABCD Camp in 2005. It was just a quick hello, and I was in a few workouts with him. I also met his brother Reggie that week, and we continued to stay in touch.

I later informed Reggie that I was moving to Las Vegas to work at IMPACT, so when he and Derrick were in town the following summer Reggie asked if I'd work with his brother. By that time, I'd started to train a lot more NBA players. Derrick was the number-one high school player in the country and on his way to play for John Calipari at Memphis.

On the day they wanted to work out, we couldn't get space at IMPACT, so I met them at a small Boys and Girls Club gymnasium. There's no sugar coating what happened: Derrick was awful. We weren't five or ten minutes into the session before he was exhausted, and believe me, it wasn't because the drills were so hard.

Derrick was truly out of his comfort zone that day. When he was at Simeon High School in Chicago, the coaches kept everything in house—workouts, practices, interviews, all of it. Not only was I the first NBA trainer Derrick had ever worked with, I was the first white guy he'd ever trained with. And remember, he was only eighteen years old—just a kid.

That's part of what I love about Derrick, and a big part of what makes him so good. Here he was, the top of his class and supposedly destined for stardom, but he was so nervous about working with me that he was totally off his game. He got tired quickly, couldn't make a shot, and then got frustrated that he was leaving such a bad impression. I could see he possessed some natural physical gifts, but I gotta tell you, I was not impressed.

I assumed I wouldn't be seeing them again anytime soon, but later that day, Reggie called me and said, "Derrick feels real bad about what happened. Can he come back tomorrow?" Right away, that told me something important:

This guy doesn't back down. He wouldn't be defeated by a momentary setback. It's funny how a guy can have a mix of real humility and overflowing confidence.

The next day I saw the real D. Rose. He had a totally different mentality. He showed much better stamina; he was making shots, attacking the rim, crossing me over both ways. There were no jitters. This was the guy who everyone said was the top high school player in the country.

We stayed in touch during the season. I got to see Derrick briefly at the 2008 Final Four. As luck would have it, he signed with Wasserman a few weeks later, so I did his predraft workouts, with Russell Westbrook joining us for most of them. Derrick moved to L.A. for that summer, but his brother didn't come with him. I give Reggie a lot of credit for that. He didn't want Derrick looking over his shoulder. He wanted him to grow up on his own. So Reggie basically dropped Derrick in L.A. and told him to figure it out. He asked me to take good care of him.

When Derrick got to L.A., he was just a few days removed from playing in the national championship game. But he didn't want to take any time off. We went hard almost every day for two and a half months. Derrick can be a little shy off the court, but once he steps between those lines, he has a much different personality. He knew how talented he was, but he also knew how much net work was required to be a great NBA player. If he was ready and willing to put in that kind of time and effort, so was I.

*   *   *

Derrick has always been a terrific communicator. He's good about returning texts, staying in touch, and following through on his commitments. He wants feedback, and he has a lot of follow-up questions. He just has this hunger to learn, and he's constantly challenging me to feed it.

Derrick was raised primarily by his mother and grandmother on the South Side of Chicago. They didn't have much. He grew up in a rough neighborhood. Like a lot of kids who come out of those environments, Derrick saw basketball as his way out. Nobody had to put any pressure on him because he put so much on himself. You can't imagine what a burden that is. Yes, it motivates him, but it also keeps him humble. He often says that he is constantly in "survival mode."

His mom taught him the importance of good karma. Treat people right, show everyone respect. He's still that way. If anything, he's more humble. His mom is the same way. You won't find her wearing fancy clothes and sporting expensive jewelry. Derrick laughingly points out that, with all the millions he's made, she still shops for discounts at Walmart and Target. His success hasn't changed her, so it sure won't change him.

Derrick was fabulous in Chicago, easily winning rookie of the year. He flew me out often to work with him. At the end of the season, I sat down with his brother Reggie to map out a plan for the future. Derrick had played really well in the playoffs, but there was much room for growth. Reggie wanted me to spend more time working with Derrick, which was, of course, great with me. The more we talked about it, the more we decided it made sense for me to move to Chicago full-time. Reggie said I could keep working with Wasserman's other clients as long as I was available for Derrick when he needed me. I was single at the time, and I knew a great opportunity when I saw one. I didn't need to be convinced.

We worked all summer in Los Angeles, and then that fall I shipped my car to Chicago and moved into an apartment downtown. Whenever I was in town for the home games, I went to every single one. Derrick and I would work out at the Bulls' facility after practice a lot. He liked to go at night when no one was around. We'd work on the floor and study some video. The coaching staff was great to me. They were fully supportive of what we were doing because they saw the results.

It was a good hour-long drive for me to get to the Bulls' practice facility in Deerfield, but I didn't mind. I certainly wasn't going to live out there. That was too quiet for me, although it was perfect for Derrick. We spoke or texted almost every day. Often, we weren't even talking about basketball. After a game we'd go to a restaurant and grab a steak or something. Derrick always had friends or family around so we'd all hang out together.

Derrick and I became really close that year, and I hit it off with a lot of his friends. I might go to a dinner where there was a table of ten or twelve guys. Most of the time I was the only white guy there. It was kind of a running joke. I'd walk up to the table and say, "Am I allowed to sit here? Is this good? You guys got my back if someone comes at me?" But mostly, we didn't even notice it. It was just our normal life.

I give Derrick a lot of credit for how he managed all of this. He was very selective about the people he allowed to hang with him. That social aspect is extremely difficult for a lot of NBA players, but especially for someone who's playing in the city where he grew up. Derrick was a bona fide legend in Chicago. He grew up in poverty, surrounded by gangs and violence. Then all of a sudden he was nineteen years old, a huge celebrity, and had millions of dollars. Everybody wanted a piece of him. So many guys in his situation would have made bad choices because they couldn't say no.

Derrick could say no.

Don't get me wrong, he's very generous in a lot of ways. He has created foundations and donated a lot of money over the years. He's also generous with his time. I can't tell you how many occasions we were walking around Chicago and I had to pry him away from a group of people because he couldn't say no to an autograph. But in his early years in the league he made some very smart choices. It wasn't easy for him to break away from some of the guys who were around him when he was younger. If he hadn't done it, though, he wouldn't have survived.

Sometimes I'll run into friends back home who think it's odd that I get along so well with Derrick and my other clients, who are usually younger and from a different racial background. At first, when questions about it would get put to me, I was puzzled. I mean, I never feel those differences at all. Particularly the race stuff. I stopped being aware of labels like that a *long* time ago—back at Syracuse when I was one of only two or three white guys on the team. Sometimes I'll hear a person in the media say, "All these groups of people would get along a lot better if they'd just spend more time in each other's presence." Exactly. Funny thing is, nearly all the time I find myself being *more* comfortable around these younger players—blasting rap, cutting up, doing whatever they're into.

That habit of hanging out with athletes of wildly different backgrounds and giving each other grief about whatever, making them laugh—it never feels forced. I've often had dinner with John Wall's family, and I'll be the only white person at a table of twenty people, and I'm having a blast. John's mom and I get along great.

This is the beauty of basketball. It seamlessly brings together people of different races and cultures. Because of my involvement in this game, I've traveled all over the world. I can't tell you the last international trip I've taken that I've had to pay for. The ball doesn't care about the color of the hand that shoots it. If you shoot it properly, that sucker will go in.

*   *   *

If Derrick had any doubt that I was committed to his success, that first season I spent in Chicago erased it. Besides working him out regularly, I went to most of his games and watched all of them on TV. I'd send him video clips to point out things I was seeing. And I was in constant communication with B. J. Armstrong, his agent, as well as his coaches with the Bulls. We were all on the same team—Team Derrick.

Derrick was comfortable enough with me that sometimes he'd call just to vent. He could be vulnerable with me about his doubts, his frustrations, and his insecurities. That meant a lot. I don't think he was someone who trusted people easily. He's very careful about intruding on other people's space. To people who don't know him well, that can sometimes come across as aloofness.

During his first year in Chicago, Derrick averaged 16.8 points and 6.3 assists and was named rookie of the year, but he had a glaring weakness: he shot 16 for 72 from three-point range. I remember watching him play against the Celtics that season in the first round of the playoffs. He scored 36 points in the opener and averaged 19.7 in the series, which the Celtics won in seven games. But I could see the Celtics defenders backing off him, almost daring him to shoot. That's what happens when you get into the playoffs. Players get scouted really well, and games tend to slow down and are played more in the half-court. So even though Derrick had a great season, I could see this was a problem that was only going to get worse.

Intellectually, Derrick understood that he needed to add more outside accuracy to his game, but it's hard to break the habit of thinking *I can drive by everyone. Why do I need to work on jumpers?* This was before the NBA went three-crazy, but things were starting to move in that direction. Nowadays, if you're an NBA point guard and you can't make threes consistently, you're probably not going to last very long.

So the following summer, we got to work on developing Derrick's range and efficiency. For him, shooting was mostly about repetition and confidence. I didn't want to change too much with his shot. It's not like it was broken. It was just a matter of getting him those perfect reps and giving him a few different moves to try. We practiced a lot of change-of-pace, hesitation moves that led to pull-up jumpers.

I told Derrick I wanted to start by working primarily on his midrange stuff, around fifteen to eighteen feet. My individual workouts have progressions, from simple and easy to complex and difficult. I also chart a progression path over the course of weeks and months, even years. I figured if Derrick could get his form down for midrange jumpers, then it would be easier to extend it beyond the three-point line—eventually.

Also, I've always believed that the elbow area on the floor is a great place to be proficient. I call it the "kill spot." It's the only place on the court a guy can't get double teamed. You have space, you can drive in either direction, you can get to the rim, you can take a one-dribble floater, a side dribble and fadeaway jumper . . . the options are endless from there. This is where I emphasize the basics of shooting. *Spread your fingers . . . elbow in . . . release at eleven o'clock . . .*

Derrick could get mad at himself pretty easily. If he went through a couple of sets and missed a lot of shots, he'd yell and boot the ball to the other end of the gym. I tried to start him off with some easy drills to get his mind right. If he started off shooting poorly, he could be in a bad mood the rest of the workout—which would make it even less likely he'd find his rhythm. It's hard to get in a good shooting groove if you're mad. The most important muscle is between the ears.

He made some gradual improvements, but it's one thing to do it in a practice gym by yourself, and quite another to carry that over to the actual games. It could be pretty frustrating to watch him play that second season. If he missed his first few shots, he'd stop shooting. He'd revert to "pass first" point guard mode. It's not like his coaches were telling him to play that way. He did it to himself. I'd try to tell him, "We just spent four months working on your shot. If you're not gonna shoot in games, we wasted our time." Sometimes he listened, often he didn't.

Even so, Derrick had a phenomenal second season in Chicago, making the All-Star Game for the first time. His three-point shooting got better, but not by much: He went from making 22.2 percent as a rookie to 26.7 percent. I'd text or call and say, "Keep shooting, keep shooting," but he wasn't confident, and if you're not confident as a shooter, you're dead.

Having seen some benefit from working on his jumper, he came out west the following summer and really attacked it. He was training in Las Vegas with the Team USA that was competing in the World Cup during the summer of 2010, and in between those sessions we got in our net work. He brought incredible urgency to those sessions. Even if I told him to take a break, he didn't want to be off for more than a day. He really wanted to keep the momentum going. It's crazy, isn't it, how long this takes? It was two full years for the top pick in the draft to learn to be a consistent three-point shooter.

When he got to training camp that fall, a reporter asked Derrick if he thought he could be league MVP. He matter-of-factly answered yes. That statement caused some waves. People thought he was being boastful, which he wasn't—that's not Derrick. He was being honest, and he pointed out to the reporter that if he was asking the question, he must also think it was possible.

He made a big improvement as a three-point shooter, to 33.2 percent. In fact, he got better in all facets and *was* named league MVP. It was awesome to see all that net work pay off. In early May, I was doing some workouts in Saint Monica's, and between sessions I checked my phone and saw that I had like sixty texts. I'm thinking, *Uh-oh, what happened?* Turns out that Derrick had thanked me during his MVP acceptance speech. Everybody I knew was giving me a high five. It was a really, really cool thing to do, and I appreciated it deeply.

*   *   *

Derrick was an awful eater when I first met him. The sports-writers in Chicago used to laugh when he'd down a bag of Skittles right before the game. I mean, the guy literally did not eat a salad until his third year in the league. Of course, it was a Caesar salad, which is the most fattening salad you can eat, but it was a good first step.

I busted his chops about it, because I know you just can't keep that up and perform at peak capacity. He'd come in for a morning workout and be worn out. "What'd you have for breakfast?" I'd ask. Lots of times his answer was nothing, or he'd report that he went to Jack in the Box on his way to the gym. On game night he'd sit in the locker room and eat a big gyro with French fries an hour before tipoff. After a year or two in the league, he figured out he couldn't do that anymore.

His diet may have been a disaster, but one thing Derrick never did was party like crazy at night. Sure, he'd go out from time to time, maybe hit a club once in a while, but he was never a big drinker. If we went out to dinner, he might have a glass of wine, but nothing more. He was always mature in that regard. He was a man on a mission, and he wasn't about to let alcohol, drugs, or bad nighttime habits derail his single-minded pursuit.

Derrick can get down on himself, like anyone else. Don't think because a guy has been voted MVP and is one of the best players in the world that he can't get frustrated. If anything, Derrick can be *too* hard on himself, because he's thinking, *If I really am one of the best players in the NBA, why am I playing like this? Why can't I make a shot tonight? Or this week?* I tried to tell him, "It's an eighty-two-game season. It's not a big deal. The great ones miss fifteen shots in a row and still shoot the sixteenth."

Derrick was terrific again during the 2011–12 season. He averaged 21.8 points and 7.9 assists and was named an All-Star starter for the second straight year. The Bulls had high hopes entering the playoffs. That's when disaster struck. I was on a plane to L.A. when I got a text from Jalen Rose that read "Sorry about your boy." That's how I learned Derrick had torn the ACL in his left knee during his first playoff game. I was crushed.

It was almost a year before we could work out again. When he came back, I was real nervous. This was new territory for me, and I didn't want to do anything that would mess with his rehab. I spoke often with B. J. Armstrong and the team doctors to see what I could and couldn't do with him.

While Derrick sat out the 2012–13 season, we eased our way back. I emphasized that he needed to let me know if he was feeling overexerted or experiencing any discomfort. The doctors who did his surgery said they'd never seen leg muscles like his. That meant he should have been able to recover quickly, but I was worried because Derrick was always the kind of guy to push through pain. He really needed to appreciate the importance of being restrained in this situation. This was his *body* we were talking about. He couldn't let his competitive pride work against him.

This is another example of how important trust is in the trainer-player relationship. Derrick was equally worried about me. He knew if something went wrong, I'd have to answer for it. So he was protective of me, too.

Derrick made his return to the NBA for the start of the 2013–14 season, but he tore the meniscus in his right knee in late November. He had to have surgery again. His season was over. Unfortunately, he has continued to suffer multiple injuries in the years since. The Bulls traded him to the Knicks in 2016. Getting traded from his hometown team, the team that picked him first in the draft, hurt him real bad.

I'll never forget sitting with Derrick and trying to encourage him to stay positive. Even when things continued to go south on him, Derrick in his soul never lost that confidence. "I know it's gonna come, Rob," he told me. It was a quiet confidence—call it faith, even. He knew he still had greatness in him, if only he could stay healthy long enough to tap into it.

Unfortunately, his lone season in New York ended in early April when he had to undergo yet another surgery to repair a torn meniscus. He played half a season with Cleveland before being traded to Minnesota in March. He did pretty well with the Timberwolves in the playoffs and the team re-signed him to a contract at the end of the 2017–18 season.

×　　×　　×

Professional athletes tend to change teams a lot, and even when they're with the same franchise they often play for different coaches and executives. So for a player to have one guy as his personal trainer over a number of years can be stabilizing. When I talk about the need to have close relationships with my clients, Derrick is as good an example as there is. No matter where he is in his career, no matter how bad things get, we're always talking.

Derrick has told me that he likes to see me still working out with young kids, which I'm still doing. That's a luxury he never had when he was growing up. You'd think that might make him resentful, but he likes that I still enjoy teaching the game, and that it doesn't matter to me if it's a future Hall of Famer or some young kid who's just trying to make his high school varsity. I see Derrick with his son—the way he cares for him and talks to him about pursuing greatness—and I know that he gets it. He's not angry about how tough he had it as a kid. He's appreciative of what he has now. There's a fine line between having a chip on your shoulder and being bitter. I don't think you can successfully pursue greatness if you're doing it out of bitterness.

In today's game, it's really hard to survive if you're a guard who can't make threes. Sometimes Derrick and I will look at games he played early in his career, and he'll notice how often he landed out of balance. The difference is that back then, he was so physically gifted he could get away with it. Now, after four knee surgeries, he can't just blow by these young guys. Maybe he's not quite as strong in his lower body as he used to be, but he's a lot more flexible. He's learning how to stretch better, he's doing yoga, he's really paying attention to his body. All of that could end up prolonging his career and allow him to live a long, healthy, pain-free life after he's done playing.

Of course, I wish Derrick's injuries had never happened, but even if he'd stayed healthy, he would have lost much of his explosiveness as he entered his thirties. The adjustments made in the wake of those injuries could very well make him a better basketball player in the long run—or at least, a more fundamentally sound one. Instead of driving by and dunking on people, he'll have to learn to shoot more fadeaways and floaters, and lots more threes. When Michael Jordan was in his late thirties, he couldn't jump over everyone, but he was still unstoppable because his skills were so good and his mind was so advanced. I can see the same thing happening with Derrick.

There are a lot of positives to going through struggles. In Derrick's case, being forced to take a step back was probably helpful. For so long he was totally wrapped up in chasing the game. Sitting out for a while enabled him to develop more fully as a person.

I started to notice this change when he had his son, R.J., in 2012. He had a daughter in early 2018. Having kids has given him something way more important than basketball. Derrick had to grow up a lot faster than most people. When I was nineteen, I was hanging out at frat parties. When he was nineteen, he was a multimillionaire celebrity with more pressure than I could possibly imagine. So many people were counting on him while he was just trying to play ball.

That's why it burns me when I see media and fans criticize him. I see what he went through every day mentally and physically with his rehab. I can't imagine what it's like to go from being an MVP to playing for three teams in two years. Then again, he's always been grounded. After he left the Cavaliers, I'd be around the team and all the executives and coaches and scouts would come up to me and say, "How's Derrick, man?" He was only there half a season, but they got a sense of who he is. Ask anyone who's played with him or been around him, and they'll tell you he is the most humble, real dude you could ever meet. Doing net work with him has never felt like work.

* * *

When Derrick came out to L.A. again in the summer of 2018, he was stronger and more free of pain than he'd been in a long, long time. He had a couple of buddies who'd traveled from Chicago with him and rebounded for us. Sometimes he'd bring his son. But there was no big entourage with him. He just showed up and went to work.

Honestly, I couldn't foresee the season he'd have with Minnesota. For most of the 2018–19 season Derrick was near the top of the league in three-point percentage. Think about that! During his first nine seasons in the NBA he made 29.6 percent from three-point range. In season number ten, he was over 40 percent. The leap felt sudden, but it had actually happened very slowly—so slowly that for much of the time even Derrick and I couldn't see it coming.

I've heard about how Derrick has been taking Karl Anthony Towns under his wing in Minnesota. I'm proud that Derrick has never taken a shot at a teammate in the press or on social media. Teams underestimate the importance of having veterans in their locker room to help the young guys adapt to the NBA's crazy, stressful lifestyle.

One night, I drove from my home in Providence to see the Timberwolves play the Celtics in Boston. After the game I was standing in a hallway with Derrick when Jayson Tatum, the Celtics' young, talented rookie, came by. Jayson approached Derrick, gave him a bro hug, and said, "What's up, O.G.?" That stands for "original gangster." It's an expression of respect from a young star to an "old" veteran.

"Do you realize how these young guys look up to you?" I asked Derrick. "You're this generation's Allen Iverson. They all grew up watching you and wanting to be you. I hope you can appreciate that because you're the one who worked so hard."

Derrick is a humble guy. He doesn't take compliments easily. He knows better than anyone that, as good as things can be in this game, they can change in an instant. But he smiled at me anyway. After all he'd been through, he was still letting 'em know.

CHAPTER FIVE

SLOW IS QUICK

One day I was driving to Saint Monica's when I realized I'd forgotten my key to the building. So I hustled home to get it . . . and discovered movers carrying my couch out of the apartment. When I tried to protest, they shrugged and said they were just doing their job.

Apparently, my girlfriend had decided to leave town without telling me. I knew we were having issues so I shouldn't have been surprised. I was actually more pissed about losing the furniture, which was hers in the first place. Plus, she took the dog. At any rate, I couldn't stay and argue too long because I had to hurry back to work out Jason Kapono. My life in a nutshell.

I'd made an arrangement with the Wasserman guys that I'd train their clients in the summer and move back to Rhode Island for the winter. So I finished out the summer (I slept on an air mattress in the apartment, since I didn't have much furniture left) and continued my training after I got home.

My years with Wasserman gave me the chance to meet a lot of players and add to my own reps on the floor. It also gave me insights into the various skills and personalities of NBA players. For a time, Jalen Rose was coming to the gym pretty regularly. He'd been retired for a couple of years, but he was contemplating a comeback. I was a big fan of the Fab Five. I even had Jalen's jersey in my room. Jalen had a lot of things going on in his life and, well, let's just say that he wasn't in playing shape. I think he realized after a few weeks that he was too far away from being ready, and at that stage he wasn't willing to put in the time and effort to come back. You can't go halfway with this stuff.

It's hard to convey just how great someone's physical condition has to be for that person to be a professional athlete. By any normal standards, these guys are in amazing shape. But there's a huge difference between being in great shape and being in *game* shape. Most of the movements and cuts you make in a basketball game can't be executed on a running track or at a Gold's Gym. You can run on a treadmill for an hour or cover lots of miles on a cross-country course, and you still wouldn't make one move that you'd make a hundred times in a basketball game. The game requires lateral movement, quick-twitch muscles, jumping off one or two legs, and lots and lots of explosive bursts.

Running in basketball isn't just about long-distance stamina. A player probably only runs a couple of miles in the course of a single game. It's not fluid running, it's a lot of stopping and starting. That's why a lot of people come to me thinking they're in excellent condition, but it doesn't take long for them to get exhausted.

These are some of the fastest humans on the planet, but there's a difference between track speed and basketball speed. Basketball is more about quickness, which is used in small, tight spaces. To be a great basketball player, you have to have burst—and that must be deployed at the exact right time to be effective.

In other words, slow is quick. This is one of my big themes. If you watch great players, they take it slow and then *Bam!*—they're by you. They're not just coming at defenders full speed all the time. Michael Jordan was great at this, especially later in his career. He'd lull guys into waiting on him and then drive by in a flash. Chauncey Billups was another player who achieved success in this regard. He wasn't naturally explosive like some other guys, so he had to learn to do it old-school.

Maybe the best all-time was Tim Duncan. Even his facial expressions were slow. His tactic was to calculate, measure up his defender, wait until the right instant, and then spin off his man along the baseline for an easy deuce. People would always say, "Oh, Tim Duncan is boring, he's so slow." That's why you couldn't guard him. He was there, he was there . . . and then he was at the rim. Which way did he go?

This is a big challenge when I'm training world-class athletes. For their entire lives, they've succeeded largely because of their physical gifts. I mean, Derrick Rose and Russell Westbrook are two of the fastest point guards ever to play the game. They're a blur—with explosive first steps, which is a deadly combination. So here I am, some dude from Rhode Island who was barely good enough to walk on at college, and I'm telling them, *Yo, slow it down*. They're looking at me cross-eyed. *Slow it down? How about I turn it up?*

Going as fast as you can as often as you can works in high school and probably college, and it might even get certain players to a level of success in the NBA. But if they want to be truly great, they have to learn how to *play*. That means taking their time, baiting defenders into a lull, picking their spots, changing gears, sizing up situations, staying in control . . . and *then* using their quickness. That's something the great ones eventually come to understand. In the NBA, slow is quick.

✳   ✳   ✳

This has been a constant theme over the years with John Wall. After seeing the progress that Russell Westbrook and Derrick Rose had made with me as shooters, he wanted to know if he could make that same improvement. During his second season in the NBA, John shot three for forty-two from three-point range. Hey, nowhere to go but up, right?

So one day he sent me a direct message through Twitter. We knew each other a little because I'd worked with him a couple of times in Las Vegas. I'd always told him I'd love to train him. As I had in the early days with Derrick, I marveled that John could be the top pick in the NBA draft and a starting point guard without being able to make three-pointers. I was living in Chicago and working for Derrick at the time that John reached out. When the Wizards came to town to play the Bulls, John and I met in the lobby of the Ritz Carlton hotel right before he got on the bus to go to the game. I was very clear with him just how long it would take for him to develop into a reliable, consistent three-point shooter. "I need you to move to L.A. this summer and work with me five days a week," I said. "If you commit to me, I'll commit to you."

"I'm on board," he said.

You might wonder if it was an issue with Derrick and Russ that I agreed to take on John as a client. After all, they had to compete against him on the court. But that's rarely a concern. The only time I feel a little resentment from clients is if they're on the same team and competing for the same minutes. That aside, guys like Derrick and Russ honestly believe that when they're at their best, nobody is better. They also understand that this is how I make a living. They pay me well, but no one wants to pay me enough that I'll work only with them.

Besides, as you've learned by now, it's not like I have a bunch of secrets. I'm just there to help them do their net work.

I felt like I could help John because I recognized a lot of his deficiencies. As was the case with Derrick and Russ, he possessed pretty good shooting form. His main problems were that he wasn't following through and he was shooting on the way down. So when he shot the ball he had to fling it like a catapult. It came off as a line drive.

That's challenging for a player who's barreling downhill fast. As great an athlete as John is, it's very difficult for someone to be going that fast, stop on a dime, pull up for a shot, and release at the top of his jump. It's equally difficult to do that and then land in a balanced position. So my emphasis with John was on trying to make sure he didn't drift to his right or left when he jumped. That would enable him to shoot with consistency because he'd be doing the same thing every time.

Being able to hit pull-up jumpers in transition meant dialing back the one thing that has always distinguished John Wall on a basketball court—his speed. If he's going full bore all the time, there's no way he can be in control and shoot with balance. If he's not balanced, he can't make shots consistently. It was a subtle adjustment, but a very important one—and one that required him to change how he'd played his entire life.

I tried to stress to him the need to be patient. That's why I build with such a slow progression during my workouts. I'm not trying to jam in everything at once. If we don't take care of one small step, we don't move on to the next one. It takes a long time to get that muscle memory down.

John worked all during the summer of 2013 in L.A., just like we agreed. Then he flew me into Washington during the season. Rhode Island to D.C. is an easy flight, so we did that a lot. John likes to study video, so I'll often send him clips during the season. I can be critical, but my main purpose is to give positive reinforcement. I sent clips to show him instances when he was shooting a perfect jump shot. It didn't matter if the shot missed. I wanted him to execute the proper form and balance.

One thing I know John appreciated is that I tailored my workouts to him. Even though I'd worked with guys who exhibited similar playing styles, I never let him feel that I was just plugging him into a formula. I'm not going to have him practice running off screens and firing catch-and-shoot jumpers as if he's Ray Allen. By augmenting our net work with a lot of video review of what he was actually doing on the court, I persuaded him I was fully locked in.

Don't think that just because a guy was the number-one pick in the draft and is a great NBA player he automatically possesses high confidence—especially when it comes to a part of the game that has always been a primary weakness. You can have the best form in the world, but if you don't *believe* you're going to make the shot, you're probably not going to.

In John's mind, this was a natural progression. Even though he was always the best player growing up, he knew that at some point he'd have to become a really good out-side shooter. That's what makes the great ones great. Sure, he was the number-one pick in the draft, but if he's not maximizing his potential and improving every year, even-tually he won't be good enough.

John learned right away that I'm not one to sugarcoat. If he's not going hard enough or doing something wrong, I'll tell him. Even after working with me all summer, it was a good twenty games or so before I noticed an improve-ment in John's shooting. If he got frustrated, I'd try to assure him, "It's coming, I'm telling you." But at a certain point I'd say, "You gotta figure this out. This is out of my hands." That ability to make adjustments when you're not shooting well is one of the factors differentiating the great ones from the good ones.

The most important thing I can do is to encourage guys to keep firing while they're going through this process. I always say, "FGAs . . . FGAs . . ." If John missed his first few shots, he wouldn't shoot in the next ten possessions. That would drive me crazy. It could be especially frustrating for him because he'd think, *I put in all that work over the summer. Why isn't this clicking?* I'd turn that around by saying that *because* he put in all that work, he needed to stop passing up open shots. "No matter how many you missed you have to believe the next one is going in. You put in too much work."

Most guys appreciate the feedback, but John is someone who really seeks it out. If I'm watching the Wizards and I notice something, I'll send him a text in the first half, and he'll hit me back at halftime letting me know he got it. I love working with John because he's very communicative. A lot of times he'll call me right after a game to ask what I thought. Sometimes I'll text him just to give him a piece of encouragement. It means a lot to me that I'm one of the few people he looks to hear from during games.

It's moments like that when I have to remind myself how young these guys are. John was nineteen years old when he got drafted. So even in his second or third year in the league, he was still a kid. That he lived in a nice house didn't mean he had the game of basketball figured out. One thing I've learned is that these guys really appreciate being treated like normal people—because that's what they are. They're regular people who want to get better at their job, just like you and me.

There's never a single moment where a guy breaks through, but I do remember a big one for John during the

2017 playoffs. The Wizards were playing the Celtics in game six of the Eastern Conference's second-round series. With 3.5 seconds to go, John hit a game-winning three-pointer to force game seven, which Boston won. He'd made that shot before, but never under so much pressure.

When the game ended, John stood up on a side table and celebrated for the crowd. I was in my living room jumping on the furniture. I called right after the game and told him that those shots he'd taken for six years paid off. I also added, "I wouldn't have cared if you missed. The fact that you had the balls to take that shot shows how far you've come. It's like you were saying to yourself, 'I *deserve* to take this shot. I worked hard, and this is my team.'"

As with a lot of players, John's work habits have become better as he's grown older. He hired a personal chef and does a lot of yoga. The season puts so much wear and tear on the body, not just the games but all the practices, workouts, weight room sessions, and travel, and enhanced nutrition and stretching are meant to compensate for that. He's also working on parts of his game like post-ups and floaters that he knows will be needed toward the end of his career when he doesn't have the same explosiveness. I've drilled into him the idea that you can be "slow" but still effective. He's far from slow right now, but he's gotten a lot more cagey, using changing speeds to make his bursts that much *more* effective.

A lot of people don't realize the pain that John has played through. Many nights after a practice or game he'd go home and have to get ice and therapy. He never complained, and he never made excuses. In our workouts, I'd try to caution him sometimes to take it easy, but he didn't want to hear it. It was as if he were convincing himself he was 100 percent when he clearly wasn't.

He eventually had surgery in the spring of 2016, and it was a good year before he felt like his old self again. But during that recovery phase he was still playing. Can you imagine how frustrating it is for a guy with his competitive pride to be out there but not be at his best? He had to have surgery on his left knee again two years later. So it hasn't been easy.

One thing I really admire about John is that he takes his leadership responsibilities seriously. That's a big reason the Wizards love him so much. He's fun to be around, and he's very open with his teammates. He'll walk through the arena and chat with the ushers. It's not as if he just puts his head down and leaves. He's very approachable. I've seen him stop after bad losses to take pictures with kids.

Unfortunately, things took a turn for the worse for John during the 2018–19 season. In late December, he injured his heel and was lost for the remainder of the season. He later took a fall at home and ruptured his Achilles tendon. So he'll be sidelined well into the 2019–20 season. I know how frustrated John is because he's put in so much net work, but whatever happens, I'm confident he'll continue to pursue greatness with the professionalism he's always shown. I have no doubt he'll fight his way back, just as Derrick Rose did. John is too good, and he works too hard, for it not to happen.

*   *   *

Another guy I've worked with who's a great example of the benefits of playing "slow" in the NBA is Al Horford. Now there's a guy who's always under control. Even his jab steps are slow. But he's a sneaky good athlete. He'll lull you to sleep and then slip right by you. He's not super quick, but he's a quick jumper, and he's great at driving with both hands. That really slows up defenders, which in turn makes Al seem faster.

Al doesn't have quick-twitch muscles like Russell or Derrick—who does?—but he has a lot of energy. He can go hard all day. I often have to tell guys that if you're going to be a pro you have to live like a pro, but I've never had to say that to Al. He sleeps right, eats right, practices right, each and every time. He's respectful to everyone and takes good care of people. He was like that even when he was playing in college at Florida. That's a credit to his parents, Tito and Arelis. It helps that Tito played a few years in the NBA with the Bucks and Bullets. Al grew up knowing that there was more to being a pro athlete than what happens during those two hours on game day.

I first met Al in the summer of 2011 after he'd switched over to Wasserman. He'd already played four years in the league and was coming off back-to-back appearances in the All-Star Game. I'd always loved Al's game. As a fan of basketball, I tried to lock in on him, because even when he was playing in college at Florida he wasn't usually the biggest star on his team. But he is one of the smartest players I've ever seen. He's always one of the best—if not *the* best—passers on the floor at any time. It's no coincidence that he's won wherever he's been—two NCAA championships at Florida, Eastern Conference finals appearances with the Atlanta Hawks in 2015 and the Boston Celtics in 2018.

Al came out to L.A. and we hit it off right away. He's not a naturally intense guy on the outside, but don't let the smooth taste fool you. He is a tough competitor and truly wants to be the best. He came to me with a specific goal in mind: He wanted to improve his offensive game. There is a difference, however, between *improving* and *expanding*. All his life, Al had been one of the biggest players on the court, so naturally he was taught from a young age to play close to the basket. By the time he started working with me, he'd pushed his shooting range back to the elbow area. So we started where he was comfortable. Al had a lot of confidence in his game, as long as it was within certain parameters.

When we started working out, Al was making all these fifteen- and seventeen-footers and I was thinking, *Wow, this guy isn't missing.* It wasn't long before I started pushing him back behind the three-point line. I always assume that anyone with sound fundamentals can become a good three-point shooter. It's a natural progression, right?

Not to Al. "You're the first person to tell me to shoot threes," he said.

"You're still a four man," I said. "That's who you are, but this is something you can definitely add. You're good enough."

What did I see? Simple: The ball kept going in. He had really good form, but even if the form was bad I probably wouldn't have messed with it much. His jab step was really smooth, which meant he could create space without being overly quick. Everything was effortless. I don't think he'd ever really worked on shooting threes before.

Nor was there much evidence to suggest he should. During his first four years in the league Al made a grand total of three three-pointers (on twelve attempts). Even after working with me for a summer he went back to the Hawks and shot just one three-pointer all season, which he missed. The following summer, we spent more time developing his shooting range, but it still took a while for him to carry it to the court. The main adjustment when you move away from the basket as a shooter is that you need to use your legs more. A player needs to be strong enough, first of all, but then he has to develop the habit of really bending his knees into the shot. Beyond that I didn't have to do much tweaking of his technique. I emphasized that he should bend his knees and explode through his hips when he went into his shooting motion, and from there just let his natural instincts take over. Nothing was broken here. It was just a matter of getting those perfect reps.

It's important for me to give guys as much confidence as I can—but it can't be false confidence. If they're not good enough, I have to tell them that, even as I assure them they'll get there in time.

Al is a very thoughtful, intelligent guy, and he appreciated my honesty right off the bat. During one of our first sessions, we were going through our usual progression of moves and something about Al was just off. I'm sure in his mind he was going hard, but he really wasn't. He was dragging. So after about fifteen minutes, I stopped.

"I gotta be honest," I said. "You're not going hard enough, and you're not getting better here. You're wasting your time. We're gonna start again from the beginning."

To this day, Al mentions that as the moment he knew he could trust me to tell him the truth, even when it's unpleasant.

Al is one of the best players I've worked with in terms of taking what we've practiced and bringing it to the games. I'll never forget the night during that first season when I watched Al play a game against the Magic. A few hours before the game, he'd asked me to come to a shootaround to work him out after practice. I went onto the court and we did some midpost jab moves. Basic stuff, but something we'd recently added to his game. It was important to get that work in because he was going to be guarded that night by Dwight Howard. That's not a guy you can easily bully at the rim.

So the game starts, and a minute into the game, Al gets the ball in the post. It was just like we'd practiced earlier that day. He turned and faced Howard, gave him a hard jab step to his right, then faded away for a beautiful midpost shot off the glass. As Al was running down the court, he pointed right at me. His mom was sitting next to me and cracked, "Wait, was that for me or for you?"

It's a long journey for a player like Al to go from the post to behind the three-point line. His high school coach used to tell him to get inside, but Al was far and away the best player on his team, so he shot some long balls just for fun. Once he got to Florida, however, he listened when Billy Donovan said he needed to be around the basket. He was so good down there, and the Gators had plenty of perimeter scorers. It must have been the right advice because Florida won back-to-back NCAA championships with Al in the lineup.

The question was whether Al could demonstrate to his NBA coaches that he was good enough to move away from the basket. During the 2012–13 season, his sixth season in the NBA, Al asked me to come to Atlanta to work with him for a week. After one practice, Al asked me to come onto the court and put him through some shooting drills. Usually our routine was to come back at night, but sometimes Al wanted to get his work done right afterward. He'd had a light practice, so we went real hard. Pretty soon we were being joined by his teammates Joe Johnson and Josh Smith. It's always a better session when you have a small group like that.

A lot of the players and coaches were still lingering around. Al put on quite a show that day. I bet he made thirty-five out of forty from the three-point line. I looked over at the Hawks' coach, Larry Drew, and saw this look of amazement on his face. You could see the wheels turning in his mind.

I was happy with the progress we were making, but I could sense tension developing with the Hawks coaches. I honestly didn't want to step on anyone's toes, but I did have a job to do. I heard later that one of the Hawks assistants wasn't happy. I can't say I blame him. The whole notion of players working with outside, basketball-specific, full-time trainers was new to the league. I wasn't well known at all. Fortunately, I'd had a previous relationship with Coach Drew because I'd trained his son a little bit in the past. Larry was fine with my being there, but more important, Al made clear to the team that he wanted me there. That was the end of that discussion.

Rick Sund, the general manager of the Hawks, was one of the first in that organization to encourage Al to become proficient at the corner three. Rick said Al could play like Sam Perkins. That philosophy continued when Rick was replaced by Danny Ferry and Drew was replaced by Mike Budenholzer. They were both very supportive of Al's expanding tools. Not only was he good at long-range shooting, but the NBA was starting to move in the direction where big men would be asked to do more of that. You can't overstate the impact that Budenholzer had on Al's development as a player. It didn't matter if Al went through cold stretches. Budenholzer told him to keep firing. It's easy for me to tell a guy "FGAs, man, FGAs," but for a coach to do that when he knows his job is on the line, that took some guts.

The progress made Al a quicker player. When he set ball screens, instead of always rolling to the hoop he was able to pop back and shoot long jumpers. His bread and butter was still his inside game, but adding the three to the mix opened up a whole new world for him. There aren't many centers who are capable of guarding a guy eighteen feet from the basket. If they tried closing out on him too hard, Al would be able to pump fake his defender and blow right by. So his adding this dimension really opened up spacing for the team.

This is why Al is a great example of a player who is quick by keeping it slow. He has a great first step and generally has little trouble getting by his defender, but the thing he prizes most is being in control of his body. That makes him quicker because he's not wasting motion. There's not much value in being quick if you're expending energy and movement in ways that don't get you a bucket.

In his case, becoming a better outside shooter made Al even quicker. Why? Because when you can shoot the long ball, the defender has to get close to you, which means you need less explosion to get by him. Throw in Al's smarts, and now he becomes one of the fastest players in the NBA, all while looking as if he is moving in slow motion. If you're always a threat to score, then you can keep the defenders on their toes—which makes *them* slower.

You might not guess it about Al, but he's pretty hilarious. Our personalities really meshed. In the summer of 2012, I went with Al on a trip to the Dominican Republic. That's his father's native country, and Al was going there with his family to do a bunch of clinics. I flew down there by myself. Tito had suggested I get a rental car because I was going to be running some of the kids' clinics separate from Al. I got the car and tried to use the GPS navigation on my phone, but it wasn't working too well and it wasn't long before I was lost. I found myself driving on all these dirt roads, and the neighborhoods I was going through didn't look very safe. I couldn't get a good signal on my phone, and I didn't speak the language. A drive that should have taken less than an hour ended up taking more than three. Suffice to say, that was the last time I drove around the D.R. by myself.

I worked out Al a bunch of times that week and did some free clinics for underprivileged kids in various cities around the country. At night we'd get some dinner and have a few drinks. It was really a fun trip.

It was a blast watching Al blossom as a three-point shooter those last few years in Atlanta. During the 2014–15 season he shot 11 for 36 from behind the three-point line. The following season he shot 88 for 256, a 34.4 percent clip. It's not a coincidence that he made the All-Star Game during both those seasons after a four-year absence, although that absence was partly the result of injuries. The increased production was timed perfectly with his free agency in the summer of 2016. Al was very much in demand and ended up signing a four-year, $113 million contract with the Boston Celtics. Now *that's* what I mean by seeing your net work pay off.

Next time you watch the Celtics, lock in on Al for a few possessions. You'll see what I mean by slow is quick. He does all the little things well. He'll make the pass that leads to the assist that creates the bucket. He'll help get a stop on defense, but not necessarily with a block or steal. He's a great team leader. You can see how all those young players really feed off him. He's probably the best passer the Celtics have right now. He also has the full green light to shoot threes.

Al is really thriving in Brad Stevens's system. He's able to make corner threes and bring the ball up the court after a defensive rebound. He's the quintessential NBA center for today's game. And wherever he goes, his teams win. Funny how that works.

CHAPTER SIX

KEVIN LOVE

On April 26, 2015, I was in Cleveland to watch the Cavaliers play in game four of their first-round playoff series against the Boston Celtics. I was there to watch my good friend and client Kevin Love. It was a big night for Kevin because he'd never been in the playoffs before. He got me a seat close to the action. We were both a bundle of nerves.

Late in the first quarter, Kevin was fighting for a loose ball with Kelly Olynyk, the Celtics' second-year forward. Their arms were locked, and as Kevin tried to jump for the rebound, Kelly yanked Kevin downward. Kevin immediately grabbed his left shoulder and ran straight off the court and into the locker room. I felt a pit in my stomach.

I was sitting in my seat trying not to worry too badly when I got a text message. It was from Kevin. He wanted me to come to the locker room. I left my seat and went down there. Kevin was trying to stay hopeful. He knew his shoulder had popped out but the doctor had reset it, and he thought he'd be able to continue to play. But he was concerned, understandably, and he wanted me to keep him company while we watched the rest of the game on television.

I saw Olynyk in a hallway after the game. I knew him pretty well because I'd overseen all of his predraft training.

He felt awful and made clear what happened wasn't intentional. "I know that's your boy," he said. "I don't know what to say." We got the bad news the next day that Kevin's shoulder would require surgery. He was done for the playoffs. Though that night is an unpleasant memory, I remember being touched that Kevin wanted me to be with him in the locker room, just the two of us. It was an illustration of how close we'd become. Our relationship is much more than just trainer-client.

I'm loyal to *all* my clients, and each one gets my full attention and energy. I'm really good friends with most, too. But there's no doubt that Kevin Love is one of my best clients and closest friends. It's the kind of bond that grows between two guys who love to be in the gym putting in hour upon hour of net work.

×　　×　　×

Our professional relationship began in the summer of 2007. Kevin had just gotten to UCLA in advance of his freshman year. Scott Garson, then an assistant at UCLA and a buddy of mine, recommended me as a way for him to get some work done away from campus. Kevin was so intense about what he was doing that sometimes it helped to get away. On Scott's recommendation, Kevin came to meet me at Saint Monica's for an introductory session.

We'd already met at ABCD Camp the year before. Something about our personalities just clicked. Kevin will tell you that I'm the only guy he ever saw besides Pat Riley who slicked his hair back. He thought it was a bold move, which, let's face it, it was. We're a couple of wiseasses who love talking ball and being in the gym. It was a perfect match.

And yet, it was *not* a great first session.

Just like Derrick Rose in Las Vegas, Kevin came to Saint Monica's way too nervous. He also weighed too much, which was even more of a problem because of his high-intensity approach to training. He was always the type of guy who had to change his shirt midway through a session because he sweated so much. That day he soaked his *shorts* all the way through. We had to keep stopping to wipe up the floor.

He missed a ton of shots. When it was over, he seemed so worn out and discouraged that I worried I'd pushed him too hard. But he came right back the next day looking for more. That's when I knew we had something.

We worked through the summer. We went out to dinner a couple of times and really hit it off. I was ten years older than he was, but we were becoming good friends right away.

Once Kevin started at UCLA, it was obvious he was going to be a pro real soon. Also on that team was Russell Westbrook, a year ahead of him, and the two were made for each other. They both prided themselves on coming early to the gym and staying late. They were so competitive that they'd try to beat each other to the weight room early in the morning.

Once that first workout was behind us, I got a feel for Kevin's skill set. The guy could really shoot. When his freshman season started, however, he wouldn't attempt many outside shots. That first year at UCLA, it was unlikely he'd be good enough to make outside shooting a staple of his game, but from the start I believed it could happen down the road if he put in the work. Kevin helped UCLA to reach the 2008 Final Four, where it lost in the semifinal to Memphis. Then he got picked fifth in the draft by the Timberwolves. He went to Minnesota with great expectations, and he had his struggles early on, as most rookies do. All his life, he'd been the best player on his team. Now he was playing with other great players, and he was learning that he needed to expand his repertoire of skills.

When Kevin got to Minnesota, the coaches encouraged him to try to score more away from the basket. He averaged 11.1 points as a rookie but made just two three-pointers all season. We started working together full-time the following summer. That's when our group with Russ and Derrick became a regular thing. Kevin was forced to do a lot of perimeter work, and he really had to keep up with the other guys' intensity. It didn't matter how good the three were. They always wanted to add something to their ability.

I was technically still a Wasserman employee, but Kevin was the first non-Wasserman guy I worked with regularly. Arn and B.J. were great about that. As long as I was available to their clients when they needed me, they had no problem with my picking up extra work. You might think there'd be some concern about my helping other players around the league get better—players who could compete with Wasserman clients—but Arn and B.J. never voiced any of that to me. Neither did the other players. Everyone in the NBA is just trying to work hard and get better. It's more of a brotherhood than a cutthroat competition.

Thanks to those three guys, I became more confident as a trainer. There was literally never a single time when I called out a drill and someone asked, "Why are we doing this?" If anything, Kevin would want *more* instructions from me. He was extremely detail oriented. He wanted to make sure he knew exactly where he was supposed to step, and how he was supposed to shoot. Kevin understands that basketball is a game of inches. Back then, he also knew that he wasn't quite the athlete Russ and Derrick were, so he had to make especially sure he was paying attention to details. At times, he can be his own worst enemy. He can be compulsive. When he was at UCLA, he used to literally count his steps as he walked around campus. There's a difference between perfecting your craft and being a hyper-perfectionist. Kevin was always one to put a lot of pressure on himself. It's part of what makes him great, but it's something he's had to be careful not to overdo.

All three guys really wanted to become more versatile. They wanted to concentrate on their weaknesses. Russ and Derrick would post up Kevin, and he'd try to beat them off the dribble and score on pull-up jumpers. The only true constant was that they had to go hard every time, all the time. The guys would call each other out if they noticed any slippage.

My workouts don't involve a lot of planning, but they're pretty organized. We do a bunch of sequences on one side of the court, take a water break, then do the same sequences on the opposite side. I remember back in those days I'd send my three guys to get some water, then I'd start to say, "All right—"

"We know, we know," Russell would interrupt. "Other side." That became a running joke. Sometimes Russ would write a tweet after a workout with the hashtag #otherside. A little humor goes a long way when you're grinding in the gym.

I realized, of course, that during the summer I was only a *part* of their schedule on any given day. They were also lifting, stretching, dropping by the right grocery store to grab some healthy food. Basketball isn't a career, it's a lifestyle. You can always do little things to get better, especially during the summer. The season is for refinement, but the summer is when you can build something substantial. The discipline comes when you decide between what you want now and what you want *most*.

Kevin likes to say that basketball is like a drug. His coach in Minnesota, Kevin McHale, often told him to "chase the game." That's why he loves working out on Sundays, because he knows a lot of guys use that as their day off. While they're at the beach, he's in the gym. It gives him his mental edge.

The progress during Kevin's second season came slowly, but it did come. Sometimes I'd get a call from him after midnight. He'd voice his frustrations, and I'd try to calm him down. "You work harder than anyone. It's going to happen," I said. "I don't know when, but if you keep having this attitude it's going to take a lot longer. Stay positive."

All that net work eventually paid dividends. Kevin attempted 106 three-pointers in his second season (up from 19 as a rookie) and made 33 percent. The following year he shot 41.7 percent from the arc on 211 attempts— and made the first of his five All-Star Game appearances. And the following year, Kevin accomplished the ultimate by winning the three-point contest at the NBA's All-Star weekend in Orlando. He framed the jersey he was wearing that night and sent it to me as a gift. It remains one of my truly prized possessions.

*   *   *

A great deal of Kevin's improvement came as a result of changes he made in the way he ate. Despite all the energy he burned off on the court, he was still a little chunky coming out of high school. The college training table isn't a good place for guys like him. Some players don't have to worry about that as much, especially when they're young and their metabolism is high. Even when we worked out at Saint Monica's, Russell might chow some fast food right beforehand. It never fazed him.

Kevin was in the league for a good three years before he started to appreciate how critical his diet was to his success. He's now the most disciplined guy I've ever seen when it comes to food. In 2014, he invited me to join him and a few friends on a trip to watch a Cowboys-49ers game. It was a party to celebrate his twenty-sixth birthday. He got us a private jet. When I walked into the cabin, I saw his buddies from home chowing down fried chicken and pizza. Kevin got on board and he was carrying a cooler. I thought maybe he'd brought us some beers, but when he opened it, he pulled out a kale salad with tomatoes. I'm thinking, *Man, it's his birthday, if there's one day he could just cut loose and eat whatever he wants, this is it.* I can't say he stuck to the program throughout the entire day and night, but at least he had the discipline to start it off right. "Marginal gains," he calls it.

Kevin has worked with top-level nutritionists to keep his habits optimal. You might think the key to losing weight and being in shape is always to eat less, but he was surprised when he went to a nutritionist who told him to eat *more* calories. The trick was eating the *right* kinds of carbs— oatmeal, yams, rice. Eating at the right time of day also became important. Kevin was so compulsive about it that he'd set a timer so he knew when to eat.

I remember when he was picked to pose for the body issue of *ESPN the Magazine* in the summer of 2015. He was already focused on being in good shape, but it became even more important to him when he knew he'd have to pose naked. He was obviously proud of how he'd remade his body. I've never seen a guy as dialed in as Kevin was when it came to food. There were times during workouts where he'd almost pass out because he hadn't had enough to eat. But eventually he found the right balance, and it has helped him enormously.

Even when we're off the court, Kevin and I always have a blast. I can't really explain it; we're just a couple of idiots together. One of my favorite experiences was when he invited me to accompany him to Asia during the NBA lockout of 2011. A lot of players were looking for ways to make money with overseas appearances. Kevin has a shoe deal in China, so he did one day of appearances there, and then we spent the rest of the week in Manila. Kevin paid me about twenty grand out of his own cut to help him with clinics, which was very generous of him. He's very well known in China. He played in a charity game and there was a big crowd.

We stayed at the Fairmont in Manila. We decided we'd just go out the first night and relax the rest of the week, but of course we ended up going out every night. We had some security with us and a couple of people who were around, but mostly it was just the two of us. That trip was also a little odd because there were a lot of rumors Kevin might get traded. We were a long way from home so it was hard to stay on top of the news.

I'm not going to lie, it's fun being out with an NBA player, especially if he's well known. Those guys are very well taken care of. They get the best seats, the best tables, and often they eat and drink for free. It's great for a restaurant's business for an NBA player to be there, so they get treated right. When I'm with them, I get treated like them. That week with Kevin, we were just a couple of guys supposedly working but actually having a lot of fun. That's how it always is with us, though—the work never feels like work.

×   ×   ×

Everyone knows that in today's NBA a straight-up post player is going to have a hard time surviving. I can't say that

I encouraged Kevin to make improvements on his long-range shooting because I saw where the game was headed. I just saw that he had a real ability that could be developed over time. Kevin saw this trend happening before I did. He was initially intrigued by Dirk Nowitzki. Kevin knew how hard it was to guard a player of that size who could shoot, because he often had to guard Dirk.

It was an evolution not just for Kevin but for his coaches as well. When he first entered the league, he was told that his game was fifteen feet and in, and that he should focus on getting every offensive rebound he could. He knew he was capable of something more. During his first couple of years in the NBA, I'd fly out to Minnesota to spend a couple of weeks with him. We did a workout one day after practice with his coaches Kevin McHale and Kurt Rambis watching. When Kevin started hitting threes, they got really excited. Kevin already had excellent shooting mechanics, so I emphasized to him the value of following through and staying in balance. He had a habit of finishing too low—finishing at nine o'clock rather than the optimum eleven, which resulted in a flatter shot. You can do that in the midrange, but it becomes a problem from behind the three-point line.

When people who follow the game talk about elite basketball players, they're always evaluating their "athletic ability." I think that's overrated. Kevin reminds me a lot of Paul Pierce. Paul didn't necessarily blow by people and dunk over them, but nobody could guard his stepbacks and spin moves. Kevin studied Pierce very closely. He's tried to copy his patented move where he dribbles one way, spins back the other, and lays it in with his opposite hand. It was kind of funky when Pierce started it, but now the whole league is doing it. His stepback was slow, but he never got it blocked.

When Kevin was traded to Cleveland in 2014, it was a huge adjustment. He was on the perimeter almost all the time, and he was clearly a complementary player to LeBron James. Kevin went from averaging 25.9 points and 12.4 rebounds in his last year in Minnesota to 17.5 and 10.4 during his first year with the Cavs. The attention directed toward him was much higher because there was so much pressure on LeBron to deliver a championship to Cleveland. All that net work, all that sacrifice, all that waiting felt worth it when it finally happened in 2016. I was at Oracle Arena the night that the Cavaliers clinched the title. After the game I went into the locker room and held the trophy with Kevin. We got a picture together, which is another one of my favorites. It meant the world to me that Kevin wanted to share that moment.

×   ×   ×

Needless to say, Kevin's life changed dramatically when he joined the Cavs. It forced him to sacrifice a lot, but he was a true professional. When you're playing with LeBron James, you're going to be a target. Kevin was the new guy on the block, so when things went wrong, he got a lot of the blame. I thought it was amazing how he dealt with all of that. He could have popped off to the media or written a bunch of stuff on Twitter, but he stayed dialed in the whole way, trying to be a good teammate and find ways to improve.

He also had to change the way he played. He was already developing his shooting range and his midpost game, but with the Cavs he became a real spacer. He learned to make corner threes and pick-and-pops in transition. All the while, he had to learn to be efficient on fewer shots. It took some adjusting, but he understood his role and accepted it.

Look, Kevin is a competitor. It's not easy for someone who's wired that way to go from being selected as an All-Star to being a role player on his own team, even if it's only because you're on the same team as LeBron James. That can hurt a guy's ego. Trust me, Kevin can be very headstrong. He can be stubborn and temperamental. It's a big part of what got him to where he is. Playing alongside LeBron, he showed, though, that you can be both headstrong and open-minded—if you're truly all about winning, that is. If you look around the league these days, you see a lot of players causing headaches in the locker room and the front office because they don't like their roles, even if the team is winning. And remember, the Cavs signed Kevin to a $150 million contract. He could have just said, "Hey, I've got my money," and not cared as much. But that's not who he is.

Kevin is also smart enough to understand how these things work. Everyone knows LeBron is great. So if the team loses or goes on a bad streak, LeBron's not going to get the blame. Don't get me wrong, it's plenty stressful being LeBron, too, but Kevin's awareness of sports being a drama with various roles having to be filled helped him deal with a lot of BS that came his way. He worked very hard on his game, and I know that LeBron respected it.

And who would have guessed that Kevin would make the critical defensive play on Stephen Curry in game seven of the 2016 Finals? Kevin got caught on a switch and had to check one of the greatest three-point shooters in the history of the league—and he came through beautifully.

Playing alongside LeBron with the Cavaliers, Kevin went to the NBA Finals four straight years. That's a lot of wear and tear on the body, and especially the mind. So we dialed back his workouts quite a bit during those summers. When we did work out, it was at a more moderate pace. We were more about refining his habits. He'd pick my brain about what I saw from him during the season and what was happening around the league, but it was certainly not the same type of intense net work as when we started out with Russ and Derrick.

In March 2018, Kevin published a first-person story in *The Players Tribune* under the headline "Everyone Is Going Through Something." It started with a vivid description of a panic attack he suffered during a game and went on to describe some struggles he's had with anxiety. I had no idea the article was coming out, and I didn't know that Kevin had been dealing with these issues. Part of me wondered why he wouldn't share that with me, but that was the point of his article. He just didn't want to tell anybody.

I called Kevin to tell him how proud I was, and to let him know that if he ever wanted to talk about that stuff I was there for him. I know he got a *lot* of calls from people at that time. What Kevin did was really brave and helped a lot of people way beyond basketball. He's told me how amazed he is at the response he continues to get. Millions of people are dealing with mental health issues, and I think a lot of people mistakenly believe that just because someone is rich and famous and playing in the NBA he's immune to these things.

DeMar DeRozan wrote a similar article in *The Players Tribune* and spoke to that very notion.

I guess I'd never given it a whole lot of thought, but I can certainly see how guys in these players' situations could suffer from depression or anxiety. The pressure on them each day can be incredibly taxing even under the best of circumstances. Both of those guys came into the NBA when they were nineteen years old. I'm just glad players like Kevin and DeMar are being more open about this, because all of us need to realize that there's another level to what's going on between the lines—and, often, outside the lines.

Kevin has become interested in mindfulness and meditation as a result of all of this. It helps him on the court, but it's also helping him prepare for life after basketball. He comes to the game with such a pure love. When it becomes a business, and when he allows the pressure to get to him, the joy can disappear.

The reason Kevin and I work so well together isn't that I know so much about basketball. It's that I know how to make him laugh. It's like we have this secret language. We bust each other's chops all the time. He loves to tease me about my days as a PE teacher by cracking, "They say those who can't teach, teach gym." (No offense to the gym teachers out there. It's a noble profession.) Ours is a bond that's really hard to find anywhere, not to mention someone you work with—or work *for*, technically. Our shared love for basketball cuts across everything.

I'm really grateful that I've gotten to be so close with a man with so much talent and great character. When my son, Rob V, was born in 2015, I asked Kevin to be his godfather. Kevin is one of my best friends, and I know that he's a great example, to me and my son, of how success depends on being true to yourself and putting in your net work—while also making time for a few laughs along the way.

CHAPTER SEVEN

ON MY OWN

It's no accident that some of my clients are my closest friends. I can't have jerks in my gym. That place is sacred, man. I don't want anyone there who's going to bring down the energy and goodwill, or someone who doesn't work as hard as the other guys.

In 2011, Jeremy Tyler came to one of my workouts. He was only nineteen years old, and he had a lot of pressure on him. He'd earned a fair amount of attention by saying he was going to skip college to play professionally in Israel. Arn Tellem had signed him, so it was my job to get him ready for the draft.

We didn't click. He had a lousy attitude, and he asked too many questions about why I was doing things this way. Let me tell you, I've worked out some of the greatest, and not one has ever asked me *why*. There's a certain level of trust that gets rooted from the outset.

But it wasn't there with Jeremy, which presented an awkward situation for me. He was Arn's client so I didn't want to piss him off, but if I let too much slide then I wouldn't be doing my job—and I wouldn't be doing Jeremy any favors, either.

Things deteriorated, and pretty soon Jeremy and I were getting into it. Will Perdue, who'd been working on the other side of the gym, came over to step in. At seven-foot-one he had three inches on Jeremy. "Don't talk to him like that," Will snapped. Jeremy went right back at Will, asking him what he'd ever done. I remember Will's reply: "You mean, besides my four rings?"

I worked with Jeremy for about a year, but then we were through. I actually felt sorry for the guy. He wasn't a bad kid—but he was a kid. Like most teenage basketball prodigies, he was used to having his ass kissed. He has since made some brief appearances in the NBA but has spent most of his career overseas. I wish him the best and I hope he has matured, because he definitely had talent.

The more clients I picked up, the more perfect reps I performed and the better I became at my craft—just like the players. I still wasn't all that organized. I didn't build charts and fill notebooks full of ideas. I did what I've always done, which is watch a lot of basketball. I recorded as many games as I could and spent a lot of time on Synergy, an analytics website that offers great video capabilities. My main goal was to isolate moves that players were making in games, and then give them an environment to repeat and groove them, and eventually build on them.

When you're working long-term with players, it can be challenging to keep things fun and fresh. You don't want anyone getting bored, including the trainer. That's why I like to work with small groups. It allows me to set up little games. *All right, we're gonna take five three-point shots from these four spots. That's twenty shots. Whoever gets the most wins.* It wouldn't be unusual for things to degenerate to a three-on-three or full-court game. If they got desperate for an extra body, I was more than happy to join. Generally, I'm not a big fan of guys playing pickup in the summer but you gotta have some fun or everyone burns out.

The 2011–12 season was busier than usual for me because the league was hit by a lockout, which canceled sixteen games. Things got even more complicated for me that winter because my dad was dying. He'd been battling cancer since the spring of 2011. He was in bad shape during predraft season, but I was afraid to miss too many workouts because I didn't want Wasserman to find someone else.

That fall, a bunch of Wasserman clients went to Hawaii for a USO tour. I was supposed to go with them to work out the players during down times. On the day I was supposed to leave, however, my sister called to say my dad had gone back into the hospital and was in really bad shape. I bailed on the trip, which allowed me to be by his bedside when he died in November. He was sixty-five.

My dad was a loving guy, but he was like a lot of men of his generation. He served in the army and rarely told you his feelings. I could call him and tell him I played against Michael Jordan and he'd say, "That's good. Anything else happen today?" After he died, I went to his house because I was looking for a tie. I went through his dresser and found two full drawers containing articles about me. I had no idea he kept them. Some were from my high school games, and my days at Syracuse, but another batch concerned the success I was starting to have as a trainer. My dad rarely told me he was proud of me, but I always sensed he was. Finding those articles proved it.

Getting back to L.A. was the best therapy for me. I kept busy for six weeks running an intense series of workouts until the NBA finally ended its lockout on Christmas morning. I was pretty worn out by then, and I only got about three slow months. Then it was back to the draft.

Meanwhile, I continued to attract more and more clients who were outside the Wasserman family. I finally went to

Arn and B.J. in 2013 and told them I thought it was best that I went out on my own. They were really cool about it.

It was definitely a scary move. I'd enjoyed a steady income and benefits with Wasserman. It was nice getting a paycheck every two weeks. Leaving that required a big leap of faith that I could continue to get my own clients and build a real business. The players I was already working with didn't have to pay me when they were with Wasserman. I'd spoken to enough of the guys that I felt confident most would stick with me.

The flip side to breaking away was that it would allow me to call around to all of the agents I knew and offer my services. I rang up big-time guys like Rob Pelinka, Jeff Schwartz, and Dan Fegan. Most were eager to help me—and their clients. I was gratified that people appreciated my skills, but it was more important to me that they believed I had integrity. If in the past I'd been trying to influence their clients to sign with Wasserman, they wouldn't have wanted to do business with me now. Not only have I learned the importance of net work, I also work hard at developing my personal and professional network. It's not just about knowing a lot of people, it's about having a reputation for conducting yourself a certain way. Whatever industry you're in, everyone knows everyone. And the only assets that really count are your skills and reputation.

I loved my time at Wasserman, but leaving ended up being the best decision of my life. Once I was on my own, I was ready to set up shop, build my client base, and get to work.

×   ×   ×

I've seen firsthand all the ups and downs that come with being an NBA player. Yes, these guys are well compensated for what they do, but it's hard to describe the amount of pressure they're under year after year. They have a lot of people, including family, invested in their success, and every season there are new people coming after their jobs. Unless you're an All-Star-caliber player, you can never be truly secure. And even if you have a very successful career, it's usually finished by your early to mid-thirties, which presents a huge mental challenge.

I don't consider myself blunt or rude, and I don't play motivational games. But I do pride myself on being honest. I think that's something my clients respect. Many of these guys have had their butts kissed since they were thirteen years old. They've been flown around the country by AAU coaches, transferred high schools a couple of times, been recruited hard by big-name college coaches, were drafted into the NBA, and become rich and famous beyond their wildest dreams. But once they enter the league, it smacks them in the face how hard it is to stick. So they realize they need people to hold them accountable.

That's why I don't tolerate guys canceling workouts at the last minute or showing up late. I let them know it's not acceptable. If I kept showing up late, they'd fire me, right? If they're late to a game or a practice or a flight, they're fined a few grand. All I ask is that they show me the same respect. Maybe some trainers are fine with players showing up *whenever*—hey, they're paying, so what's the difference, right? It's like they're afraid to lose clients. I've never been afraid to lose anyone.

Of course, as rigid as I am about punctuality, I've never been rigid about workout planning. When I first started, I mapped out a lot of stuff. But then when we actually got on the court, I'd switch things up. I always want to be attuned to the energy in the gym. I like to make changes on the fly, adjust the tempo, keep my guys on their toes. If I try something and sense it isn't going well, I'll stop. I learned early on to trust my instincts.

I might come in with a general plan, but a lot of times when I'm doing a drill, I'm not really sure where I'm going next. If the player isn't making shots, I'll make an adjustment to get him in a rhythm. I want my guys to be challenged and to learn to play through misses, but it's not helpful to have someone missing ten shots in a row. In those cases, he's likely to get overly frustrated and lose focus.

The biggest mistake I made early in my career was pushing guys too hard. Part of it was because I didn't know any better, but I'm sure part of it was also my desire to impress them. The problem is, a lot of my work with NBA guys happens over the summer. They don't need to get real worn down. I eventually learned that it wasn't smart for them to go into NBA training camp in peak condition. It was better to be about 85 or 90 percent of the way there. This was especially true for guys who played deep into the playoffs. Their season might not end until late June. They didn't need to be killing themselves in July to prepare for training camp in October.

*   *   *

Of course, every player responds differently to work, and over the years it's been fun to drill a wide variety of players and observe the range of responses. Here are a few of the guys I've worked with and what we learned during our net work:

- **J. J. REDICK**. When I first started working with J.J., he was only a year removed from college and was still trying to find his place in the NBA after battling some injuries. Contrary to his reputation, J.J. wasn't just a catch-and-shoot player. He could do a lot of stuff off the dribble, so I gave him a ton of reps doing just that. I admired his work ethic, too. Yes, he had that reputation as a "punk" when he was at Duke, but to me that's just a guy with a competitive edge—and believe me, you need that in the NBA, where you're competing against not just your opponents but also your hungry-for-minutes teammates.

J.J. was serious about his net work. There were a couple of times we were scheduled to meet, and for whatever reason Saint Monica's was closed. We always found another gym, including one time when we drove around the neighborhood and found a 24-Hour Fitness. Every year J.J. came back to me he was stronger and more fit and had added something to his game.

Incidentally, J.J. Redick is a great athlete. This is another case where that word gets poorly defined. There are a lot of things that go into being an "athlete" besides dunking over people. J.J. has great footwork, balance, lateral movement, and hand-eye coordination. He's a much better defender than people realize. And he competes his ass off.

- **BRANDIN KNIGHT.** When Brandin was getting ready for the draft after his one season at Kentucky, he'd work out with a strength coach, come do an hour and fifteen with me, and then go running on the beach. Then he'd want to come back and do another session with me at night. This was every day for several weeks. I finally had to sit with him and say, "Dude, you gotta slow down. You can't keep doing this to your body. It might not catch up with you next month or next year, but in about five years it will. Your body needs to rest and recover."

Brandin replied that he'd done it that way his whole life and didn't want to stop. I had to remind him that he was about to embark on an eighty-two-game season. He needed to be smart about it. Frankly, I'm not sure that he really listened. When he was drafted by the Pistons, I heard reports that Brandin would sneak into the gym at night. This is a great problem to have, but it can be a problem. I'll predict that over time Brandin is going to have to better manage his intensity, but until then, it's clearly working for him. Old habits die hard, I guess.

- **CARMELO ANTHONY.** I've never had Carmelo as a formal client, but I've worked with him maybe ten times. Being a Syracuse guy, I got a kick out of that, but what's really fun is watching that ball go in the basket time after time. When you work with Carmelo, you can just tell the rebounder to stay in one place. In his prime, Melo could body people and dunk on them, and he could also step out and shoot threes. He is as offensively gifted as any player I've ever been around. He's a little older now and his body is beat up, but he's still getting more than his share of buckets.

- **DION WAITERS.** A lot of younger guys come into the league thinking they're working hard but wind up learning otherwise. It doesn't make them bad people, it just makes them inexperienced. Dion Waiters is a player I'd put in this category. When I first worked with Dion, he was still in high school. He'd already committed to Syracuse, and I got connected with him by a fellow alum. Dion had a lot of questions in those early workouts. He wasn't disrespecting me exactly, but he also wasn't trusting me to do what I said. He was a mix of curious and obstinate. This was early in my career, and I made the mistake of letting him affect how I managed the workouts. If he was questioning something, I'd sometimes offer to do something else. I realized later on that I should have been more confident in my direction and at some point cut off his questions. That was a good lesson for me to learn. I knew what I was doing, and I needed to project that to the client. If I wasn't confident in myself, why should I expect the player to be confident in me?

Of course, no sixteen-year-old kid is going to understand how intensely you have to work to make it to the NBA, so it was interesting for me to see Dion make that progression through high school, his one year at Syracuse, and his time in the NBA. After the Cavaliers made him the number-four pick in the 2012 draft, Dion was a little slow out of the gate, but by his second or third year in the league he'd adopted a much more consistent, professional approach. He's truly learned to appreciate the importance of net work. That's why he's having such a great career right now.

- **BRANDON JENNINGS.** There might be some players who go at it as hard as Brandon, but I can tell you that no one works harder. I'll never forget the time he was with the Pistons and they came to Boston to play the Celtics. Brandon asked me to drive up from Providence to work him out. It turned out there was a terrible snowstorm that night, but he still wanted to try. So I found a gym at a Division III school. We had to park far away from the front door and I could hardly see because the wind was blowing snow all over the place. But we got inside that gym and did a good, hard hour. The next night, Brandon had twenty-eight points and fourteen assists.

That's how it is with a lot of these guys—they need to get up their shots to feel right. Brandon couldn't *not* work out the day before a game. Joe Dumars, the Pistons' general manager, joked with me afterward that he wanted me to work Brandon out before every game the rest of the season.

When Brandon was with the Bucks, he flew me out lots of times to Milwaukee to keep working him out. I did the same after he signed with Detroit in 2013. Then he had a freak injury, somehow managing to tear his Achilles tendon without any contact. The injury was especially tragic because he was playing so well. Over the last few years, he's had a hard time just finding a spot on a roster. Brandon played fourteen games for the Bucks during the 2017–18 season but got waived by the end and is now playing overseas. This is a tough business, to say the least.

- **TYREKE EVANS.** Now this is a guy who's *really* experienced some ups and downs. He's a Wasserman client, so I've been working with him since his rookie season. I've always loved being on the floor with Tyreke because he has things in his game that I could never teach. They can seem like funky playground moves—hesitations, feints, rapid changes in direction—but they actually work in an NBA setting. As big as he is (six-foot-six, 220 pounds), he's pretty unorthodox for a point guard. He's got a long, wiry body that allows him to kind of skip through the lane, get up high off the rim, and complete a play with guys bouncing off him.

  Tyreke had a phenomenal rookie season with the Sacramento Kings. He was one of three rookies in league history to average twenty points, five rebounds, and five assists. The other three who've done that were Oscar Robertson, Michael Jordan, and LeBron James. In his fourth year, he signed a four-year contract worth $44 million. But then he had some injuries that set him back. By the end of the 2016–17 season, he was an unrestricted free agent and signed a one-year deal with Memphis for the league-minimum salary.

  Tyreke had already made a lot of money by then, so he could have easily just gone with the flow. But he wanted to get on a better path. I hadn't worked with him since I left Wasserman, but his agent reached out and asked if I'd take him on. Obviously, I was interested but I cautioned him that I couldn't have Tyreke come in two or three days a week. That's not what I do. If Tyreke would commit to going five or six days a week throughout the summer, I was all in.

His dedication was impressive. Sometimes he'd land in L.A. early in the morning and come right to the gym from the airport. He worked out consistently all summer and came back into the season in shape and full of confidence. He had a great season for Memphis, averaging 19.4 points, 5.2 assists, and 5.1 rebounds, and at the end of the season he signed a one-year deal with the Indiana Pacers for $12 million.

Everyone asked me what I did with Tyreke, but I kept saying, there's nothing complicated here. He just put in tons of hours of net work. He also made sure to eat better and take care of his body. This is what often happens over time. These players come in so young, strong, and talented that they don't have to take care of those details. Then they get a little older, slow down a tad, absorb some wear and tear, suffer a few injuries, and they realize they're not young anymore. Tyreke has worked his way through that, and as a result found his way back to good health and NBA stardom.

• **KENNETH FARIED.** This is one of the more challenging guys I've worked with. Faried, a six-foot-eight power forward for the Houston Rockets, is a freak athlete who works his tail off, but his job is to get rebounds, set screens, and run the floor. Aside from conditioning stuff, those assets don't translate easily to workouts. We'd start by doing some close-in jump shots, but I had to come up with rebounding drills and defensive closeouts to mimic what happens to him in a game.

When I get guys in a group workout, I try not to keep things separate. The guards do post-up moves, and the big men work on their perimeter stuff. With Kenneth, though, it was important to keep his shooting to within fifteen feet. His mechanics aren't terrible, but he's never really worked at it. I didn't want to spend too much time on things he'd never try in a game, and I didn't want to send him back to his team having planted the idea in him that he should attempt things his coaches didn't want or need him to do.

It's very unusual, especially in today's game, for a player to be as successful as Kenneth and not be a good shooter. He's the closest thing we've seen to Dennis Rodman in a long time. His energy on the court is ridiculous, and he's one of those guys who just has a knack for the ball. He's not just a powerful jumper but a quick one—and a quick repeat jumper. So if he misses the first rebound attempt, he can tip it to himself, and then go up and get it quicker than the guy next to him. That's not something that I or anyone else can teach him. My job was mostly to keep his legs strong.

• **ELFRID PAYTON.** Sometimes I look for guys I want to train, players who have a lot of talent but still have plenty of room to get better. I got very interested while watching Elfrid Payton when he was a rookie with the Orlando Magic. He was quick and aggressive, but his jump shot reminded me of John Wall's when he got to the NBA. It was very flat and he didn't follow through. He could shoot well but just wasn't consistent.

I rang up Elfrid's agent, Aaron Mintz at CAA, and he got me a one-week tryout. When it was over, I told Elfrid, this is something we can fix, but you gotta give me a year. We worked out all summer, and then during the 2016–17 season, when Elfrid was with the Magic, I flew to Orlando a couple of times to work him out some more. He got traded to Phoenix during the season, and I flew out there to meet him so we could work out and watch video. I told him, the idea is to become not a better shooter, but a more *consistent* shooter. If he was having an off day, he should be able to correct what was wrong without me standing there. It's my job as the trainer to teach him to teach himself.

Elfrid was pleasantly surprised by the amount of time we spent on fundamentals. He was expecting some gimmicks, but I was very straightforward. I wanted him to be tired right away so the rest of the workout would feel like a game. Being tired was no excuse for failing to do the drill the right way every time. Perfect reps, baby.

At the same time, I was very attuned to the other things Elfrid was doing to get into shape. If he was sore from lifting, we might have a lighter shooting day. If he was rested, we might go super hard. It was my job to tailor the workout to how he was feeling. And he knew I wasn't afraid to push him.

The main thing Elfrid needed was to improve his shooting range. This was familiar territory for me, but I didn't want to change his shot too drastically. He tended to release the ball a little too low, so I encouraged him to keep his hand higher on each rep. Even if a player's shooting requires drastic change, I like to break it up and have him make small adjustments over time. If you give him too much, it gets into his head.

Some of the adjusting I did with Elfrid was how he got into his shot. He tended to pound the ball a little too much. I wanted him to go more smoothly and efficiently into his pull-up jumpers while pushing down the last dribble before he shot. That helped him create more lift and better balance. Elfrid had a tendency to rush through his shots to get to the next rep. By slowing down just a little, he could achieve those perfect reps. I assured him we'd do enough conditioning work along the way.

- **BROOK AND ROBIN LOPEZ.** The Lopez twins worked out together a lot. They're both great players but have two very different personalities. Brook is more laid back, even in the way he plays. He looks like he's moving in slow motion sometimes. Robin is more intense and emotional.

  I started with them in the run-up to the 2008 draft. Those guys could be very competitive with each other, and once in a while things might become physical. They have an older brother, Alex, who is big, too. If ever Brook and Robin looked like they were going to go at it for real, Alex would come down from the bleachers and break it up. I told him, "You better be ready to do that, because I'm not getting in between those two big dudes."

  Off the court, Brook and Robin are two of the nicest people you'll ever meet. They've both made a ton of money but they're not the flashy type. Their big thing is a summer trip every year to Disney World. Those guys are obsessed with Disney. I'm not just talking about bringing their kids, I'm saying this is what they love to do. When Disney opened up a park in Shanghai in the summer of 2016, Brook and Robin flew out there for the grand opening. That's how much they're into it. I love that they're big kids. They're also into comic books and all that stuff. I don't think they go home at night and watch a ton of NBA games.

  To be honest, it's been a real challenge for those guys to keep up with the way the NBA game has changed. They can't just live in the paint and play with their back to the basket anymore. Brook is capable of averaging twenty points and ten rebounds. In 2017–18, he earned $22 million with the Lakers, but the following year he was getting a minimum $3.3 million in Milwaukee. That's how fast things are changing. Unless you're a freak like DeAndre Jordan, Dwight Howard, or Clint Capela, it's hard to be successful as a big man if you can't shoot with range. That has put the onus on me to help these guys develop that part of their games. Lately I've been working with the Lopez twins on developing their pick-and-pop moves. That's not easy considering how long it takes, and the fact that they've never played that way before. But it's necessary for their survival.

- **BRIAN SCALABRINE.** Brian was with the Celtics team that faced the Lakers in the 2010 NBA Finals. He didn't play much in the series, but the guy playing ahead of him, Kendrick Perkins, tore his ACL in game six. All of a sudden, Brian was looking at possibly playing in game seven. He was a Wasserman client, so the night before the game his agent, Bob Myers, called and asked if I'd work him out before the game just to get his juices flowing. I barely knew him, to be honest. He'd been in a couple of my groups for predraft work, but that was about it.

Brian was pumped. He was convinced he was going to hit the game-winning shot and be a legend in Boston forever. After the workout was over, we were sitting next to the court and I said to him, "Any chance you have an extra ticket to the game?"

He looked at me and said, "Are you really asking me for a ticket to game seven of the NBA Finals?"

We both laughed. It was pretty ballsy, I guess, especially considering that we barely knew each other. As it happened, I got a ticket from someone else, and the Lakers won the title. As for Brian, he only played one minute of that game. But I'll always believe that had they asked him to play more, he'd have been ready.

- **JIMMER FREDETTE.** I worked out Jimmer in 2013 following his rookie season with the Kings. That was set up by his agents at Octagon. He came to L.A. for a few weeks. That guy never got tired. It wasn't like Russ flashing around and dunking everything, but it was always *next drill, next drill.* He had a great handle and made every shot. And talk about a good kid. He loved to hoop and never questioned what I was asking of him.

  Jimmer was selected by Sacramento with the tenth pick in the 2011 draft. There was a lot of debate about whether he was a point guard or a shooting guard. I think the Kings were kind of stuck on that. My answer is he's a pure shooter. He does a very good job at slowing down and using pump fakes and hesitation dribbles to create space.

  Yet, within four years Jimmer was pretty much out of the league. This baffles me. You're telling me that it wouldn't make sense for a team that needs outside shooting to bring this guy off their bench? He's not John Paxson or Steve Kerr? At worst, he can sit in the corner, and either teams are going to have to pay attention and keep a defender close to him, or they'll lay off him and the other guys can find him.

  At any rate, Jimmer is playing overseas and making really good money with a Chinese shoe company. He's beloved over there. But I still say he's good enough to play in the NBA, and I predict he will again someday.

- **JaVALE McGEE.** The biggest thing I had to conquer with JaVale is that he wanted every move to be a dunk. I'd tell him, "Okay, let's start on the block, catch it, go one dribble, and put up a left-hand floater." He'd take one dribble and throw down a slam. I told him, "JaVale, you're not going to be able to dunk everything in the NBA. We're going to need to work on your skill."

JaVale is a hilarious dude. He's a prankster. But he always worked hard. He'd go from me to boxing to lifting. It's pretty amazing because in 2016 he was pretty much out of the NBA after being waived by the Mavericks. That summer the Warriors invited him to training camp, but there was no guarantee he'd make the team.

Now, JaVale has two championship rings. Once you have that pedigree, people really want you, which is why the Lakers signed him to a one-year deal for the veterans' minimum. JaVale's body has gotten better every year. He's ripped right now, and he's learned how to finish without dunking, whether it's a mini hook or a layup. You can't help but learn a lot when you play for a championship team.

This league is tough, man. Once you're out, it's very hard to get back in. There are 450 players in the NBA, and every year 60 more get drafted. Brandon Jennings scored fifty-five points in the seventh game of his rookie season. Last year he played in China and had to scrap his way to a spot with the Bucks. Then he got a lucrative offer to go to Russia, so he took it. Jamal Crawford was sixth man of the year a couple of years ago, and he only got a job with the Suns at the last minute. Nick Young is out of the league. So JaVale is a prime example that when you get an opportunity, you better be ready.

- **JARED DUDLEY.** I would classify Jared as a slow-is-quick guy. He's big and strong, and he knows how to use his frame to create leverage against a defender. He isn't necessarily great at anything but he's really good at a lot of things. He's an above average athlete, but he's been a great teammate everywhere he has been. If that wasn't the case, he wouldn't have played eleven years (and counting) in the league.

That's largely because he does the little things well—takes charges, defends the best player. He's a good shooter who can knock down a three once in a while. It's something you definitely want in the locker room.

My approach with Jared during training was to keep things simple. We'd do one- and two-dribble pull-up stuff, and that's about it. He wasn't the kind of player who would blow by you, but he had a nice pump fake and midrange game. Plus he was scrappy.

Jared can really talk—in a good way. When the season is over he's always doing media stuff and podcasts. I'm sure he's going to be doing that when he's done playing. That kind of outgoing personality is a huge asset to have in a gym during the dog days of July.

- **COURTNEY LEE.** After a few years I had enough high-profile players and momentum that agents would reach out to send me clients. In 2012, Dan Fegan called to ask if I was interested in working with Courtney Lee, who at the time was with the Rockets. Courtney knew very little about me, but he knew players I'd trained, and the results we got. He and I worked for a few days in L.A., had another week's worth of sessions in Florida, and then Courtney agreed to come to L.A. for the summer. Courtney enjoyed the workouts because almost every day there were other really good players around. He responded to that because he believed he needed to develop skills at game speed and against game-quality defense.

Courtney has always been a classically gifted shooter. It's what allows a guy who played at Western Kentucky to succeed for nine-plus years in the NBA. In his case, my main emphasis was to drill down on his footwork to allow him to create the space he needed to shoot a little more quickly. As the years go by, a player like Courtney loses a little bit of his quickness, so his technique has to be more precise. He can still create space for his shot, but it has to come in different directions—a jab step, push off to the side, stepback, fadeaway, floater. He has to be more adept with his weak hand, and he has to get into his shot a little more quickly.

Courtney came back to L.A. in the summer of 2016 as a member of the Knicks, for whom he'd averaged thirty-plus minutes per game the previous two seasons. At this point it's just a matter of sharpening the skills that have been in place for so long. It has been interesting to watch Courtney's overall regimen evolve. Now he spends a lot of time building up his core with pool workouts. His routine has become less about strength and more about flexibility. He knows that being a thirty-three-year-old NBA player is a full-time grind. Younger guys are coming into the league and they want his job. They're quicker, but he's smarter. He works hard to stay on top of his game.

My type of client.

CHAPTER EIGHT

CANDACE AND LeBRON

I picked up a different kind of client in 2009 when I started working with Candace Parker. She was in her second year with the Los Angeles Sparks of the WNBA and had recently had a daughter, Lailaa. Candace wanted to lose the baby weight and get back into shape for the coming season.

I'd previously worked with Candace's ex-husband, Shelden Williams, when he was a client with Wasserman. I met her when she was pregnant, and she was already working on her comeback plan. Candace is very goal oriented. Her due date was May 19, so she pegged July 5 as the day she wanted to play. My job was to make sure she met that goal.

To that point, I hadn't had much experience training women. Maybe a few high school girls, but that was it. So this would be by far the best female player I'd ever worked with. Normally, it wouldn't be that different from training a man, but considering she was coming off having a baby, it would be a steep learning curve for both of us.

Candace had dealt with injuries in the past, but she'd never had to push through this kind of change in her body. She worked out as much as she could while she was pregnant, but her core muscles were real weak after Lailaa was born. It's hard to be good at basketball with a weak core.

Candace showed up at the gym for our first workout with just herself and her infant daughter in a carrier. Obviously, I wanted her to take it easy at the start. We did some basic shooting drills and got her moving again. During that first week, her back locked up on her a little bit. It would be a slow process, to say the least.

After a while, I felt comfortable pushing her. That's what she wanted, right? That's when she developed a habit of pausing the workout to say, "I want to go check on Lailaa."

"Lailaa's fine," I'd say. "You just want a break." Not that I could blame her. It was a veteran move.

At six-foot-four, Candace is one of the best forwards ever to play women's basketball, but she's also highly skilled and likes to score from all over, including from behind the three-point line. So it was important that I tailor my workouts not just to her gender and her unique situation, but also to her skill set. That's what she saw in me when I trained Shelden. Things got a little more intense with each workout. We'd go hard five days a week with a lot of shooting, saving Saturdays for the lightest sessions. Funny how Lailaa always seemed to be okay during those Saturday workouts.

Candace later told me that she felt some pressure because she didn't want to tarnish my view of female athletes. At one point early on she said to me, "I promise I'm not usually this bad." This from a woman who'd just been named MVP of the WNBA in her rookie season. It was ridiculous for her to think that I'd be concerned, given what her body had just gone through, but that's just her competitive personality. If anything, I had to be careful to prevent her from overexerting herself to prove some kind of unnecessary point. To me, an athlete is an athlete. I know a great player when I see one.

I had just as much respect for Candace as for any man I'd worked with, but I was definitely out of my comfort zone. Usually, when I'm working with NBA guys I can talk about things I've done with past players that might be relevant to them. With Candace, I had no point of reference with other women.

Actually, the best comparison turned out to be Kevin Durant. Working with Candace was similar to working with KD. I could give her anything, and she was great at it. I was blown away by her versatility. The key was getting her to her best spots. Once we figured out what those were, it was just a matter of getting those perfect reps. If I worked with Candace in a group, I didn't limit her to just drills with post players. She was doing the same thing the point guards were doing.

She was as determined as any athlete I've ever trained. There were several times when the session was over and she'd want to keep going and I'd have to say, "No, we've done enough today." I emphasized that she needed to listen to her body. I was mindful of that core. I could tell at the start she was having a lot of problems moving laterally and pushing off. She also had trouble bending. Pregnancy, I now know, destroys those midsection muscles that you need the most in basketball.

Candace is an impressive physical specimen, but she found her success in basketball by polishing her skills. I've since learned that this is common among elite female players. In the WNBA, there aren't players like Kenneth Faried or Clint Capela, who have imposing physiques and excel at specialties like rebounding, but sometimes lack offensive skills. In the WNBA, the biggest players have to be versatile or they won't survive.

A lot of people don't realize that WNBA players basically get no off-season. They don't make a whole lot of money, so they'll often head overseas to add to their income. When I started working with Candace she was going to Russia when the season was over. She played there January through May. She brought Lailaa, sometimes nursing her at halftime of games. Right now, there's way more money overseas for female players than in the WNBA. I hope that's not the case for much longer.

In the end, Candace just wanted me to treat her like any other athlete. She'd seen how I was with Shelden, so if I was different with her she would have known it. I was the first full-time trainer she'd ever worked with, and she liked that I wasn't trying to be delicate. There was no *reason* to be. She was immensely talented and hardworking, and she talked as much trash as any dude I've ever known.

Generally speaking, I've found the women I work with to be more fundamentally sound than the men. They know how to do the small things that feed into their skills. I'm not just talking about college and pro players, either. Even the younger girls are more polished than boys. Unlike the top male players, most women are in college for three or four years. Breanna Stewart, who's one of the best female players of all time, played four years at UConn. When I'm doing predraft workouts with a man who only spent a year in college, I'm often going to start with alley-oops and hard drives just to get him going. A lot of times they don't have great skills, and frankly they don't have the work ethic because they haven't had to bear down for a long period of time yet. The game comes easy to them.

Since those sessions with Candace, I've worked with a few more female players. I spent about two weeks working with Skylar Diggins when she was at Notre Dame. I've also trained quite a few high school girls. Recently, that has included Azzi Fudd, a fifteen-year-old girl from Washington,

D.C. I started training Azzi during the summer of 2018. I'd heard from some friends in women's basketball that she was special—maybe on track to become the best ever. I'm always skeptical when I hear things like that, but I gotta tell you, I didn't doubt her for long. I went to Washington to work with Azzi and put her through shooting drills just like I do for my NBA guys. She was nailing everything. These weren't basic moves, either. I asked her to do two-dribble stepbacks, side jabs, fadeaways, long threes, one after the other. She has one of the purest shots I've ever seen. Best of all, she clearly likes to put in her net work.

That's why I love basketball. It doesn't matter what age, size, race, religion, or gender you are. A baller is a baller. Candace really taught me that.

×   ×   ×

For NBA players, the season is a real grind. People have no idea how hard it is. You're in Detroit one night, Cleveland the next, Minnesota two days later. It's the dead of winter, you're getting to your hotel room at five in the morning, sleep till eleven, go to shootaround, get ready for the game, go at it again, night after night. A few years ago the Golden State Warriors brought in a sleep specialist to help them maximize their downtime. As a result the team scheduled flights to leave much later in the day so their guys could sleep in. Every little bit helps.

I've seen the same advances made when it comes to food. It used to be the grub on the flights and around the practice facility was meat-based and high in carbs. Now these teams have vegan chefs, smoothie bars, and, in general, much better choices. Makes sense, right? You invest all these millions of dollars in your players. Why wouldn't you spend a little more to make sure what they're putting into their bodies is smarter and healthier?

Food, rest, recovery—it is all hugely important these days. I'd imagine Larry Bird could have played a lot more years in the NBA if we knew then what we know now. You hear all these stories about the hours he'd spend shooting in Boston Garden on game days, the miles and miles he'd run. I think his body wore out a lot sooner than it might have otherwise.

Most of what I've learned about this stuff has been by observing. I've never tried to become a strength coach. I'm too worried some guy will get hurt while he's lifting weights with me. I also never studied to become a nutritionist, but I've explained to my players that once you go down the route of eating right and feeling light, you never want to eat crap again.

It's pretty simple, actually—it comes down to discipline. When you go to a restaurant, do you get a burger or do you get grilled chicken? Do you take the easy way out and chow some pizza? It's not like there aren't good options out there. You can even get salad at McDonald's now. I get that it's not easy sometimes, but if it means a difference of millions of dollars, isn't the extra discipline worth it?

I don't scientifically track injuries, but anecdotally I can tell you I've seen a significant increase over the years. I think it goes back to high school and grassroots basketball. These young teenagers are playing five games in two days sometimes. Why? NBA players don't play four games in four days, and they're grown men in peak condition. It doesn't make sense to me that parents and coaches do this to young players.

Keep in mind that when kids are playing all those games in the summer, it's not like they're icing properly after games or stretching with a trainer. There's no one there to make sure they're eating the way they should and getting their sleep. I'd like to believe parents are getting smarter about this stuff, but I haven't seen any evidence.

×   ×   ×

Sometimes I hear the phrase *injury prone*, and I'm not quite sure what that means. You see someone like LeBron James go through an entire career without a major injury (knock wood), and you wonder, are his bones and tendons built differently? Or is he just lucky? Probably both. But one thing I do see is how one or two minor injuries can have a domino effect. If you have a bad ankle that you keep reinjuring, that'll cause you to compensate, which could lead to knee problems. That's why it's so important for guys to really be careful with their bodies.

Unfortunately, coaches (who are always facing short-term job security) too often push players to come back before they're ready. That's not good for the player, which means it's not good for the franchise—long-term, anyway.

The worst part about being injured frequently is the mental piece. I've seen the toll that can take with someone like Chandler Parsons, who has been a longtime client of mine. Chandler's agent, the late Dan Fegan, first contacted me in the summer of 2013 because he knew I'd trained other Florida guys like Corey Brewer, Nick Calathes, Joakim Noah, and Taurean Green. Chandler was also friends with Courtney Lee, so I often paired them together.

Chandler and I have similar personalities. In other words, we're both wiseasses, and we have no filter. He says exactly what's on his mind. Even though Chandler is six-foot-ten, he's always been a face-up shooter from long range. The main thing he wanted was to get better in the midrange. Nowadays, it seems the midrange jump shot is basically extinct, but I'm still a believer in it.

Chandler is always going to have a certain type of swagger, especially off the court. He's not cocky, but he's extremely confident. He's not fake at all. He's does some fashion modeling, he's been all over TMZ, he likes to hang out in L.A. He enjoys the life. Some guys hide that stuff, but he doesn't.

I think that made it tough for Chandler when the injuries began. He started his career with five solid years for the Mavericks, but his body gave out on him beginning in the 2015–16 season. It started with a badly sprained ankle, but then he injured his right knee and had to have surgery that March. Despite that, the Memphis Grizzlies signed Chandler to a four-year, $94.8 million contract in July 2016. He got off to a rough start in the wake of his knee surgery. Just when he was hitting his stride, he got a bone bruise on his left knee. After that, he tore his meniscus, which cut yet another season short. He continued to experience soreness the following season, and although he shot a career-best 42 percent from three-point range, he only managed to play thirty-six games.

The Memphis fans, irked by that big contract, booed Chandler early during the 2017–18 season. He got frustrated, telling the media after the game he thought it was "tasteless" and that he'd "go into every game with the mentality that it's a road game, if that's how it's going to be." Part of the fans' frustration had to do with that max contract. What was he supposed to do, not take it? That summer was just crazy. I mean, Solomon Hill got $50 million, Joakim Noah got $72 million. Mike Conley got $153 million.

Chandler and I have the kind of relationship where we talk through a lot of this stuff. When he's bumming, I usually know about it. And it's obviously not his fault that he's been hurt so much. Trust me, he tries as hard as he can to stay in shape. During our summers together, he would work out with me, then leave to go to lift, rehab, do yoga, or do whatever else he needed to get ready. Even if Chandler was only physically well enough to get up a few shots, he'd come into the gym. A lot of guys wouldn't do that. If his body wasn't right he'd let me know, but for the most part, he was always grinding his way through it. I think as the years have gone on Chandler has gotten better at listening to his body.

Most people don't see that part of it, though. Chandler basically didn't practice for two consecutive seasons, which is a killer for someone who relies so heavily on his outside shooting. I really stressed to him the need to get to the rim more, but it's not easy for someone who's coming off injuries to trust his body. Chandler knows if he drives, he is going to be drawing a lot of contact and increasing the possibility of an awkward landing. But you can't do any of this half-assed. If you're barreling down the lane in an NBA game, you have to be totally aggressive. You can't be thinking, *Do I jump off this leg or that one? How should I try to land? Where is the contact coming from?* Obviously, it's a lot easier for me to say it than for the player to do it. It requires him to go a long while without feeling any physical discomfort, so he stops thinking and starts playing.

I worked with Chandler almost every day during the summer of 2018. We had a blast. It was the first time in a long time that he was totally pain free. We could do a good hour workout. I thought he looked great, so we were both bummed when he developed soreness again in his left knee, which forced him to miss a lot of time during the 2018–19 season. Things went sour between him and the team after that. To be honest, it's been tough for me to watch. Chandler is only thirty years old, but because he basically didn't play for three years he should be able to have an extended career on the back end. But first he has to get healthy.

* * *

As the years pile up, my philosophies have changed. Some of that is driven by the wear and tear on my own body. I just turned forty in January 2019. I have to pace myself a little more now. I can't be out there trying like crazy for every drill. I work out three or four times a week, but being on the court for that many hours with world-class athletes is a great way to stay in shape. It's also a great way to get old, fast.

By the same token, I've become very careful about hanging with my guys in clubs or trying to edge my way into their scene. Not that most of my guys are partiers, but I've seen other trainers get caught up in the NBA life. That's one of the real hazards of what we do. I never want my guys to think I'm in it for the wrong reasons.

That's also why I'm not a big social media guy. Sure, I put some pictures up on Twitter and Instagram, but I don't do it often, and that's never been central to what I do. Some guys—KD comes to mind—are really private about their stuff. And I damn sure can't be doing workouts if I have a bunch of camera crews in my gym. I'm friends with a lot of people in the media, but most of the time I don't let them in.

These players are in the public eye so much, the last thing they want is to have to be "on" during an off-season workout. If I'm pulling out my phone all the time or bringing in camera crews, they'll think it's about me, when it's really supposed to be about *them.* They don't want the whole world to know what they're working on. Why tip off the competition? I don't want anything to compromise the trust between me and my clients. That trust is my lifeblood.

I gotta say, I get a kick out of the little workout videos I see online. It's one of two things—either the trainer is using some type of contraption or gimmick to show that he's really innovative, or it's a clip of the player making a bunch of shots in a row. I laugh and think to myself, *Oh, really? You made every shot, huh?* I don't mean to knock other trainers. If that's the way they want to do their business, that's up to them, and if their players are fine with it, it's all good. It's just not my way. I can't be who I am if I always have three cameras in my face during net work time.

I've been a close witness to the analytics revolution, but I can't say I spend a lot of time studying numbers. I check them out and I watch a lot of video, but that's about it. I see these people break out a ton of numbers on a guy, and I want to say, Yeah, but can he play? I know a lot of really smart people love those numbers, but I'd rather trust my eyes. I don't think basketball is that complicated.

There's a whole lot of overthinking in the predraft process, in my opinion. It's crazy to me that these teams have seen all the top picks play a bunch of times since they were fifteen years old. Then after watching them in a couple of workouts, these same teams are going to start breaking down these kids' analytics? What did these teams see from these kids when they watched them play?

That transition from college to the NBA isn't easy at all. College and the NBA are two different sports. Not two different games, two different *sports*. In the NBA the players are much faster, longer, more athletic. The shot clock is shorter, the three-point line is deeper. Different offenses, lots more possessions. You've got six-foot-nine guys playing point guard and six-foot-eight guys playing center. The spacing and skill level is just crazy.

A lot of times people will argue that a guy should stay in college so he can continue to develop his game, and for many people that *is* the better option. But there's no question that players can still improve while they're in the pros. In fact, if they don't keep improving, they won't be able to survive long-term. The best ones know that, which is why they work the hardest. They also have the advantage of being able to focus just on basketball. In college, you have many other things that take up your time. The coaches who go from college to the NBA feel the same way. They don't have to deal with recruiting or academics or any of that stuff. It's all ball all the time.

I'm always looking for new drills and ideas to keep things interesting. Stephen Curry showed me a three-point shooting drill called "Fifty." The idea is that you shoot from five different spots around the three-point line. The first three shots at each spot are freebies. After that, you keep shooting until you miss. Once you do, you move onto the next spot. The object is to have fifty makes by the time you're done at the fifth spot.

Not surprisingly, Steph is the only guy I've seen make it to fifty. One time Eric Gordon made thirty-seven in a row from the first spot—and he didn't make it to fifty. Dudes get tired. But when I tell them I saw Steph get to fifty, they sure do want to keep trying.

×   ×   ×

One night I was in Miami preparing to meet with John Wall. We were talking on the phone to set up the logistics when John casually said, "LeBron's coming."

Uh, okay.

This was during the summer of 2017. I'd never worked with LeBron James before, so it was going to be quite the experience. He walked into the gym and was all business. He didn't question what I wanted, he just asked what we were doing. We got right into it. He brought a lot of energy, and I was intent on pushing him. When I get that way with KD sometimes, we might go the entire workout without a break. After about eighty minutes, LeBron had his hands on his knees. He cracked a smile and said, "Hey, bro, you know I'm old, right?"

It meant a lot to me that John would bring LeBron to our workout. It showed how much he trusted me. All my guys work hard, but when LeBron steps on the court he really changes the energy. He just has this aura about him. Even other great NBA players, including All-Stars, can feel it. Plus, a lot of the younger guys in the league grew up watching him and dreaming of playing against him. When they get into a workout or practice situation, they don't want to let him down.

I learned a lot about LeBron by being around that Cavaliers team with Kevin Love. Kevin has always talked about how LeBron makes everyone better, not just because he's such a good passer but because he expects a lot from teammates and holds guys accountable. He's the first player in the gym and the last one out. He raises the game of everyone in the building, from the front office staff to the people at the ticket window.

The other thing that's cool about LeBron is that no matter how good he gets, he is always looking to add something new to his game. The other players really respect that about him. They know they can never really catch up to him because he's always pushing ahead and making himself uncomfortable.

LeBron is big with punctuality. If the bus is supposed to leave at nine, you better be on it at nine. Kevin told me that LeBron will tell the bus driver to take off if someone is late. Kevin has also told me that because LeBron expects so much of himself and his teammates, guys are afraid to let him down. He makes them feel that they're playing for something bigger than themselves. "People were shocked when he came back to the Cavs—not only at how hard he works but how much he practices," Kevin told me. "He really puts in his time."

It's not easy to impress and outdo Kevin when it comes to net work, but LeBron succeeded. He's also a brilliant basketball mind. LeBron could lead all the walk-throughs and do the scouting reports for his teams. He'll change coverages in an instant, and always ask the right questions. He's also into the history of basketball. When guys start talking about players from different eras, LeBron will drop a name they never heard of.

When Kevin came back to the Cavaliers, Mike Miller, who'd played with LeBron when he was a rookie, told him, "He's lost a step." *That's losing a step?* Kevin thought. LeBron had gotten so much better with his footwork and had added so many elements to his game, it's like he became quicker. He had all these different post-up moves. He could still get by people, but he wasn't relying solely on his explosiveness anymore. Like Jordan toward the end of his career, he was less quick and explosive, yet he'd become a better basketball player.

I don't get starstruck all that easily, but there's definitely a different feeling when LeBron is in the gym. He never became a full-time client, but I did work him out a few more times. Each time, it was an opportunity for me to step back and appreciate how far I've come from that court in the woods back in Rhode Island. All these years later I'm still doing net work, but now I get to do it with the greatest players in the world. I still can't believe how lucky I am.

CHAPTER NINE

KD AND STEPH

After a few years of working with all these great players, a certain momentum sets in. Word gets around that you know what you're doing, and other players want you to do the same for them. Until very recently, there weren't a lot of trainers who were specifically focused on working out NBA players. By the time that market exploded, I had a healthy head start.

After being around Russell Westbrook and watching him grow into an MVP-caliber player, his teammate with the Thunder Kevin Durant took an interest in what we were doing. There was nothing formal about it. Russ mentioned one day over the summer that KD wanted to join us. Of course, it was cool with me. There aren't a lot of players at KD's level, in terms of both talent and work ethic.

KD must have enjoyed that first session, because it wasn't long before he was coming in five days a week. We carried those sessions into the season. We'd find a two- or three-game home stand, and I'd spend that week in Oklahoma City. That would give us time to work out on his off days and generally spend time together to talk about his progress and what was going on around the league.

Kevin loves everything about the game. Mostly, he loves to be in the gym. Sometimes we'd be sitting in his town house at nine-thirty at night, and all of a sudden he'd say, "Let's go get some shots up." So we'd drive to the Thunder facility and do a hard hour-long workout. Then I'd go to practice the next day, do a shooting workout with him when it was done, watch the game, go out to eat afterward, and get right back after it the following day.

I remember one night in Oklahoma City when we were supposed to get in some net work. For some reason, we couldn't get into the Thunder facility. I asked him if he wanted to just wait until tomorrow. "No," he replied. "Let's figure this out." He made a couple of calls and we found a church gym that was about thirty minutes away. So that's an hour-long round trip for a forty-minute workout. We had no security. It was ten at night. It wasn't the greatest of gyms. The floor was a little slippery, and I was nervous. It wouldn't be a good look if KD hurt himself. But he wanted to get in his net work, and that's all there was to it.

I've worked with a lot of great players, obviously, but KD is just different. Some guys are really good at one or two things. KD is great at everything. He's seven feet tall, but he's very versatile. He's also very detailed. Just like Kevin Love, he'll ask me questions about exactly where I want him to step and how I want him to shoot. It might be only an inch or two, but that's a big difference to him. People often ask me if it's more challenging to work with such a great player, but to me it's actually easier. Whatever I ask him to do, I know he's going to be great at it. It makes for a fun time.

KD's a great example of a player who never loses his desire to get better. You could make the case that he's the best player in the world right now, but we always went into the off-season with a plan to pick an area and improve on it. KD has gotten smarter over the years about getting his rest. Playing so late into the playoffs every year as he's tended to do with the Warriors, he can't put in as many hours over the summer. He's lucky he's never gotten seriously hurt. At this point he needs to preserve his health more than anything. Yet, he'll still put in his off-season hours.

When I first met Kevin, he was young and very quiet. Once he gets to know you, though, he opens up. He's funny. He'll chop it up. I'm used to guys taking a while to trust me. There are so many people coming at them and trying to get something out of them. When you're twenty years old and you're a millionaire, things change real fast. Yes, I work for them and they pay me, but I'm not looking for anything else, and in time they figure out that I genuinely care about them.

I'm close with my clients, but I also know how to mind my own business. It was definitely strange watching all the drama when KD left Oklahoma City for the Warriors. I know Russ wasn't happy about it, but to this day I've never asked either one what happened. I try to stay in my lane.

There is all kinds of potential for conflict if you're not careful. Take the shoe companies. I know a lot of people who work for those companies, and often I know they're trying to sign one of my clients. Let's just say I'm never wanting for gear. But they all know I'd never try to use my relationship with a player to steer him one way or the other. If I just did that one time, it could be the end of me.

The main thing I've learned from KD is the importance of working with a purpose. I don't have to stress to him the idea of perfect reps. He lives that. If anything, he taught *me* how to raise my standards. I can't think of a single workout we've had where I felt like it didn't matter to either one of us. Everything he does is detailed and purposeful, with the intent of improving and translating our drills to an NBA game.

With KD, I always need to have my mind ready and active. Often, during a drill, I'm thinking about what I want to do next. He's not big on water breaks. I can come up with any kind of creative shot, and he's going to make a bunch in a row. But I better have somewhere to go when each drill is over.

It's pretty amazing when you think about it. I don't know that there's ever been a more purely gifted offensive player in the history of basketball. I'm talking about all the different ways you can score with the ball. Yet every time we're together for a summer, his only thought is, *How can I get better?*

He's a real fan of the game. A lot of players don't necessarily watch a lot of basketball. And that's fine. They eat, live, and breathe the game all day, so the last thing they want to do is watch more basketball when they're relaxing at home. But KD wants to watch everything and know what's going on in the league. We'll gossip about who likes who, and what trades and free agent signings might be coming.

KD is an all-around sports nut. As you can see, I tend to get along with guys like that. We're both huge football fans. One day he took me on a private jet and we flew to a Cowboys-Redskins game. We hung out on the field before kickoff. I'll never forget the time I accompanied him on a trip for a sneaker tour that took us through Paris, Milan, Rome, and Barcelona, among other places. We were scheduled to depart from New Jersey, but there was a problem with the private plane. We ended up dealing with a six-hour delay and had to take a different plane. Throw in the long flight to Paris (I know, I know, poor me) and we were exhausted by the time we landed.

It was late at night, and by this time Kevin was pretty annoyed, mostly because it had now been two full days since he'd had a workout. Two days! I told him it was cool, that we would get our work done in the morning, but that wasn't good enough for him. "We're gonna do it right now," he said.

Now?

So there we are in Paris, it's after midnight, and this crazy dude wants to find a gym. But where? Fortunately we had a bunch of Nike guys with us, and they scrambled to find us a place. They told me it was some school where Tony Parker once played.

We were both frustrated and jet-lagged. And you know what? It was one of our best workouts—one of the best workouts I've ever been a part of, in fact. The gym was totally empty, and right away KD wanted to get started. His energy was off the charts, especially given the circumstances. And that gave *me* a ton of energy, too. I was charging at him, guarding him, shouting at him, talking smack. The dude did not miss. I stopped a few times so he could get something to drink, but each time he shook me off and said, "Nah. What's next?" So I kept coming up with another drill, another round of shots with hardly a miss, and then asked him if he wanted a break. "Nah. What's next?"

It was one of those nights where I had to stop and say, What the heck is going on in my life? Private jet across the ocean, awake for almost twenty-four hours straight, after midnight, empty gym, just me and one of the greatest ever to play the game. That night is all you need to know about Kevin Durant. Nothing comes between him and his net work. It was also great for our relationship. Whatever happened from then on, we'd always have Paris.

×   ×   ×

In the spring of 2013, I got a call from Jeff Austin, an NBA agent whom I've known for a long time. He was inquiring on behalf of one of his clients, Stephen Curry. Steph had just finished his fourth year with the Golden State Warriors, and though he'd dealt with some injury issues early on, he was coming off his best season, finishing ninth in the NBA in scoring at 22.9 points per game and setting a new single-season record for made three-pointers. Steph had been working for several years with a trainer in Charlotte, where he grew up, but he was coming to Los Angeles to shoot a commercial and was looking to get in some extra work. Jeff asked if it would be okay for Steph to come to the gym and join my groups for a week or so.

As I always do, I told Jeff they wouldn't have to pay me out of the gate. I suggested that Steph and I just get in the gym together and see how it went. He was a promising young player for sure, but he wasn't yet the All-Star/MVP he is today—though he was getting there fast. The team also had a long way to go; the Warriors had lost to the Clippers in six games in the semifinals of the Western Conference playoffs.

At first it was just the two of us working out. Then I moved him into small groups. At one point, I put him with Shawn Marion and Courtney Lee. Steph's younger brother, Seth, joined us for a lot of workouts that summer, too, which was cool because they didn't get a lot of opportunities to work together. Steph and I clicked right away. I'd studied his game in advance and took note of how quirky he was. He made all these half-moves and side jab steps and took a lot of long shots off-balance. But that ball sure did go in a lot. With him draining so many shots, I wasn't about to change much.

It's important that I come into these workouts not acting like I know everything. If the guys see that I've done my homework before I start telling them what to do, they'll be more likely to trust me and listen. I never want to come across as a know-it-all, because I'm the first to say I don't know it all. Net work is at its best when the players and I are finding the answers together.

The first thing I noticed about Steph was how good he was shooting off the dribble. We'd be doing a drill and he'd be way off-balance and I'd think, *There's no way that thing is going in.* But of course it did, a lot. The first few times it could be luck, but when it keeps happening you can't say that anymore. That was something I'd have to get used to, because so much of the training I do is emphasizing that guys stay in balance when they shoot, and also when they land. There's a difference between being off-balance and being out of control. Steph was always in control of his body. He was excellent at shooting not only off-balance, but also off the dribble. His release was so fast I couldn't get over it. He'd pick it up and *poof!* It's gone.

I remember seeing Steph sitting with Shawn Marion for a long while one day and just talking about basketball, the league, the business, really soaking up his experiences. Steph wasn't just hiring a trainer, he was joining a community of guys who were great at basketball and loved to work at it.

For the first couple of days, I thought Steph was a little bit quiet. We'd never met before. He responded well to my philosophy of trying to make everything in the workouts mimic a game. He liked the fast pace, and my reliance on feel as opposed to mapping out a lot of technical things. I'd get him in a good flow, build up his confidence, and before he knew it he'd made ten or twelve in a row. They were all shots he takes in games.

Steph must have liked what we did, because he hired me to come to the Warriors' training camp and do another week together. Now I wouldn't say that I can guard Stephen Curry. If nobody in the NBA can, I sure can't. But that didn't stop me from trying. I'd do my best to shadow Steph and give him a taste of what he might face during a real game. I've always thought my youthful energy was one of my best assets as a trainer, so I use it as much as possible. Steph especially loved when I'd call out a countdown clock as if he were about to hit a game winner. Anything to break up the routine and appeal to his competitive nature.

Steph and I also bonded quickly in our love of the game and taste for hard work. As he mentioned in the foreword, he was blown away that after I was done going so hard with him, I'd put in another six or seven hours in the gym with other clients. That's why it's never a big deal to these guys that I wasn't some great pro player. I could never dream of having their level of talent, but we have a lot more in common than people might think. We talk about things that are going on around the league and their team, and they know I won't blab about it to others or post stuff on social media. When we're in the gym together doing our net work, it's a pure experience. I make sure to keep it that way. Basketball is a universal language, and it connected all of us.

I knew Steph had ankle problems, so I had to be very careful about how hard I worked him at first. The last thing I wanted was to make that worse. It's easy to forget now, but after his first couple of years in the league there were a lot of people questioning whether Steph's ankles could hold up. It can be tricky when a lingering injury gets into a player's head. It took time for him to trust those ankles again.

When the season started, I could see many games where he seemed afraid to make a particular move or jump off a bad ankle. I've seen that too many times. Once guys stop trusting their body, their confidence goes way down. Once Steph got fully healthy and confident in his body, he took things to another level. He was finishing at the rim with confidence, committing fewer turnovers, and throwing better passes. His shooting percentages were ridiculous. In 2015, he won his first MVP award.

It's interesting because as humble as Steph is, you can see on the court when he's feeling good about himself. He does those shimmy shakes with his shoulders that drive some people crazy. I don't see a big contradiction there. Mostly, he's just having a whole lot of fun. He's not the kind of guy to walk onto a court and talk a lot of trash. He's more subtle about it. He's not a yeller and screamer, but he'll get forty on you real quick.

Technique is important, but the most important factor when it comes to that area of the game is feel. Steph has that in his genes, since his father, Dell, was one of the best shooters in the NBA when he played. Once that feel is ingrained, it's just a matter of getting perfect reps to build muscle memory. You look at guys like Klay Thompson and Ray Allen. Their form is absolutely perfect. They're both really hard workers, too. Ray was extremely meticulous with the way he trained. Even the way he dressed off the court, how he always matched his socks with his tie—that kind of attention to detail permeated everything he did. He had the same routine for every shot, every practice, and every game. No wonder he was such a clutch shooter.

You might be thinking, well, Stephen Curry is maybe the best player in the world. What could I possibly have to teach him? It's not that I have these great secrets to convey. What he's looking for most is a true partner, someone who respects him but isn't afraid of him and who's always willing to challenge him. He mentioned in the foreword the time we were in London and I wouldn't let him take the day off. At that moment it was my responsibility to remind him what it took for him to get this far, and what it'll take for him to stay on top. And of course, once I got him in the gym, he went hard, not because he had to but because he wanted to be there.

*   *   *

Right about the time we started working together regularly, Steph was being courted by all the major sneaker companies. Under Armour wanted him bad. I had a buddy who worked for that company, and one day he sent me about a dozen boxes full of gear. I never said a word to Steph but I did wear the gear. Heck, if someone sends me stuff, I'm gonna wear it. As I like to say, "If it's free, it's me." At one point Steph cracked, "I see what you're doing there," but of course I'd never try to sway him one way or another. He signed with Under Armour a few weeks later, but I assure you it had nothing to do with me.

Obviously, Steph is one of the most talented players in the NBA, as well as one of the hardest working. But his biggest contribution to the Warriors is the culture he has been able to create. Everything that is happening at Golden State is a direct result of his dedication, humility, and character. He's selfless, he's great with kids and fans, and he's very genuine the way he shares the ball. Think about it—this guy was the go-to shooter on a team that won seventy-three games and an NBA championship. He was unanimously voted MVP. Yet he gets on a plane and flies to the Hamptons just so he can convince Kevin Durant to sign with the Warriors. Steph knew that would mean he'd get fewer points and fewer shots. He could have said, "Hey,

I'm the man here, we just won a title, we don't need anyone else." But he didn't. He thought KD could make the team better, so he was all in. Believe me, a lot of superstars in the NBA wouldn't have done that.

It wasn't long before I was traveling pretty regularly with Steph. I spent a lot of time in the Bay Area while we worked for two full seasons. Once the Warriors started going deep into the playoffs, we spent less time in the summer because Steph needed his rest, especially when you throw in his USA Basketball obligations.

I'll never forget our first trip to Asia. I rode on the private jet with Steph, who was just coming off his MVP season, as well as Kris Stone and Kevin Plank from Under Armour. You might think I was pinching myself through the whole trip, but if anything I had to remind myself that I was with an international superstar, because Steph seems so normal to me. He doesn't ever give you that BS celebrity ego treatment. It's just like when I'm hanging with my boys from Rhode Island—except we were on a private jet.

Things got pretty crazy once we landed. We had security, but there were people everywhere. In situations like that Steph can be too good a person. He'll start signing auto-graphs for everybody. Finally, the security guys stepped in and told him, "You gotta go. You can't sign for two thousand people." They really love him in China.

I'm older than Steph, of course, so I enjoy talking about NBA history. His dad played in the league so Steph's famil-iar with prior eras. He's also very hands on with pretty much everything in his life. Whether it's basketball, family, or business, he's not a big delegator. Even when he's doing his camp, he's there the whole time and very involved with the kids. He's there at 8:00 a.m. and he leaves at 7:00 p.m. That doesn't happen with everyone's camp, believe me.

Steph comes across to the public as being as normal as a guy can get for a superstar, and I'm here to tell you he is. He used to tease me that my complexion matched my bright white socks. There's a lot of downtime on those Asian tours. There were times when it would just be me and him on a private jet for a really long flight. So it went well beyond just trainer-client, which is how it is with a lot of my guys. I just can't stress how humble Steph is. That means he's always going to get better because he'll never feel like he has done enough. He loves and respects the game too much for that.

Being around guys like this will always keep me humble, too. I've been able to generate some success in my profession, but I'll never think I've got it all figured out. I'll never treat people poorly (including and especially the "little people"), and I'll never stop working to get better. I've learned a lot from guys like KD and Steph about how someone can keep his edge but stay grounded. People are always so worried about being ruined by failure, but I think it's more important not to be ruined by success. As much as I'd like to think I've helped KD and Steph get better at what they do, I truly appreciate how much better they've made me, too.

CHAPTER TEN

INSIDE THE NBA

As I've mentioned, when I was at Wasserman I worked for an agent named Bob Myers for several years. I enjoyed being around Bob because as hard as he worked, he never took himself too seriously. He was Arn Tellem's right-hand man, so he was a big-time guy, but Bob was a lot of fun and never made me feel unimportant.

I could relate to Bob's humble beginnings in basketball. He started off at UCLA as a walk-on, but unlike me he earned a scholarship as a sophomore. That was the year the Bruins won the 1995 NCAA championship. Bob actually got some decent playing time his last two years at UCLA. We got along great because we both just loved being around the game.

In 2011, Bob left Wasserman to become assistant general manager of the Golden State Warriors. A year later, he was promoted to GM. Bob isn't the only reason the Warriors have since grown into an NBA dynasty, but he has certainly made a lot of the key decisions. Despite all of that, Bob is still the same old hoops-loving gym rat he's always been. He even still plays in weekly pickup games. You can go to a Warriors practice, and before the players arrive Bob is out there balling like he always has.

That tells you a lot about the Warriors and the culture that Bob has built and thrived in. It is a professionally run franchise so they have their rules and procedures, but you'd be surprised how laid-back things are around that place. The coaches and front office people want the players to work hard when they come to practice and the games, but they also want the guys to be happy. That feeling of being part of a group that gets along isn't always easy to achieve, but if the culture emphasizes it and keeps things in balance, it can lead to a lot of winning.

The Warriors are a great example. They don't have any jerks on that team, just good people who love to do their job, as Bill Belichick likes to say. Anyone can be the man on any given night. Steph Curry won the league MVP in 2015, but Andre Iguodala was named Finals MVP. You think Steph cared? Neither do I.

That culture starts with ownership. I remember seeing Joe Lacob and Bob Myers at a Big East tournament game one day in New York. When do you ever see the owner scouting a college game? That shows how invested Lacob is in the team's success. That commitment feeds down to the players. When they know the owner is all in, they don't want to let the guy down.

I really believe the players on the Warriors like each other. There have been a lot of times when I'm supposed to meet Steph for dinner, and he shows up with several of his teammates. I'm not saying all players have to like one another all the time, but if a team doesn't have these fundamental bonds it's going to be hard to function on the court as a true unit. The Warriors don't want jerks on their team. It's an unwritten but closely followed rule.

But what about Draymond Green, you say? Surely he's a jerk, right? Actually, wrong. Every team needs a guy like

Draymond. He fills the role that Charles Oakley and Dennis Rodman used to play with Michael Jordan's Bulls. Those guys burned hot, and sometimes they overheated, but that passion came in handy during the course of a long season. Draymond's teammates know that in the end, Draymond just wants to win. So they put up with whatever comes with that.

I happened to be at the Staples Center the night Draymond and KD got into an argument in a loss to the Clippers early in the 2018–19 season. As a result, the team suspended Draymond for one game. Everyone made a big deal of it, but I don't think it really hurt the team. Tempers get hot in the NBA, and it's not uncommon for teammates to go after one another. It's just that in this instance, it happened on national TV, and it happened to the one team that everyone is most interested in. Teammates are like a married couple. They fight sometimes. Obviously, you don't want that going on every day, but if a franchise has a proper culture in place, it can handle that kind of open conflict once in a while.

Steve Kerr fits in well there, to say the least. He's one of the funniest guys I've ever been around. He's animated and likes to enjoy himself, but he never makes it about him. He also lets his guys play, which shows he trusts them. Any good coach will tell you that players win games in this league. The coach has to have a system in place, but in the end the best ones put the game in the players' hands. You can't overcoach, and you can't get on them too badly for missing shots.

I think being a longtime former player really helps Steve relate to his guys. When the team is on a road trip, he's happy to have them take a day off and go play golf or something like that. You very rarely see Steve yell real loudly at his players. He's much more into positive reinforcement. Maybe college coaches have leeway to get on their guys like that, but pros tend not to react well to an overbearing coach.

Brad Stevens is another example of a coach who can command the respect of his players without doing a whole lot of yelling. I first got a taste of what Brad is all about when I was working at Wasserman. I was traveling through Indiana and wanted to take a trip to Butler. I was impressed with how they achieved back-to-back NCAA championship games, so I wanted to see what I could learn by visiting. I reached out to Brad, and even though I didn't know him at all, he got right back to me and said to come on out.

I showed up at Hinkle Fieldhouse in Indianapolis, and Brad sat down and talked to me for twenty minutes before practice. I took notes the whole time, not so much on his drills as on his demeanor. I don't think he yelled out of anger once during the two days of practice I saw. It was all positive. That's when I realized this guy could coach in the NBA. I knew he'd be able to handle coaching younger guys who were super wealthy, because it wouldn't ruffle his ego.

Of course, I couldn't have guessed that pretty soon he'd be coaching the Celtics. Even if I see him after they lose a game by thirty, he'll stop and talk and treat me as well as he treats anyone else. I go to the Celtics' training camp every year. Before practice, Brad comes over and greets everyone who's there. He's the same humble guy he was at Butler.

That's of a piece with the broader culture in Boston. It's no accident that through the decades this has been one of the most successful franchises in all of sports. Danny Ainge, the Celtics' general manager, reminds me a lot of Bob Myers. He works real hard but he has a laid-back demeanor, and he treats everyone like family. He has hired a lot of good people whom he trusts, and there's a real spirit of collaboration. That's big when it comes to culture. If you have one leader who has to be in control *all* the time, everyone else in the room is thinking, *Why are we here?*

Mike Zarren, the Celtics' assistant GM, is a good friend of mine. He's a Harvard grad and he does a lot of the number crunching with respect to the salary cap and the collective bargaining agreement. Mike is a lifelong Celtics fan, and when he was growing up his family always had season tickets. When he goes to home games now, Mike still sits in those seats high in the upper section of TD Garden. The guy could literally watch the game from anywhere he wants, but he'd rather be up high with the fans. That's the Celtics for you.

×　　　×　　　×

People would be shocked at how infrequently NBA teams practice. Once the regular season starts, a team might practice two dozen times—total. Between games, travel, and the need for rest, there's just not a lot of time for drills and going over offensive sets.

One of the challenges of being an end-of-the-bench guy is the need to stay in game shape. Unfortunately, the best way to do that is by playing in a game, so if players don't get in the game they have to make sure they're getting in extra work. Sometimes they'll do a forty-five-minute session before the game, but often they'll work out after the game if they didn't get major minutes. The whole point is to be ready for the moment your name is called. Nowadays players might get sent to the G League if they're not getting much playing time with their NBA club. I know that can be a blow to their competitive pride, but there's just no way to simulate the conditioning required to play in an

NBA game. If the G League is the only place you can get it, then you better go get it.

The mental part is the most challenging aspect of riding the bench. It's very hard to be patient and persistent when you're not getting minutes. You might not get called to play until game seventy—but you better be ready. You might only get one opportunity your whole life. We've seen it in football with a guy like Kurt Warner. In basketball, the best example is Jeremy Lin. He bounced around to a ton of different teams, and the Knicks weren't even sure they wanted him, but when they were forced to play him because there weren't enough bodies, he shined. He didn't just go out there and pass the ball and try to fit in. He made something happen. That's a great lesson for all of us.

All of this puts an even higher premium on having coaches who can communicate effectively with their players. That only happens if there's a real connection. If you look at the NBA coaches who are succeeding today, you don't see them going crazy on the sidelines or getting in guys' faces. Maybe that was the way things were twenty years ago, but the assumptions are different now. It's a players' league. They make the most money, they have the most power—and everyone knows it. A twenty-one-year-old multimillionaire doesn't want to get yelled at in a condescending way in front of twenty thousand people. That doesn't mean a coach can't criticize his guys, but he better have a good relationship with the player he's criticizing or it won't go over well.

Another coach I've gotten to know and really respect is Erik Spoelstra in Miami. I met Spo in the run-up to the 2008 draft. The Heat had the second pick so they were the only other team besides the Bulls to work out Derrick Rose. At the end of the workout, Erik asked if he could put Derrick through a few drills. They did some easy ball-handling and zigzag drills, and then we all went out to dinner.

Spo and I have kept in touch ever since. I think a big reason we connect is that, just like with Bob Myers, we relate to each other's roots in the game. Spoelstra was a pretty good player at the University of Portland, and after playing professionally in Germany for a couple of years he got hired as the Heat's video coordinator. There aren't a lot of highly successful NBA coaches who started off as the video coordinator for that same team, but then again, there aren't a lot of Erik Spoelstras.

Spo is a cool customer and a straight shooter. It's hard to imagine how difficult it was for him after LeBron James and Chris Bosh joined Dwyane Wade in Miami. Of course, you want to have the best players on your roster, but typically they come with a lot of distractions and drama. Yet Spo kept his composure, and he was never afraid to let the players—including LeBron—know that he wasn't taking any crap.

When the team got off to a rocky start in the first month, people were already saying Spo should be fired. Remember the incident where LeBron looked upset about something and bumped the coach on his way out of a time-out early that season? Spo, who at that point was just forty years old and starting his third season as an NBA head coach, never lost the team. I think it's because he knew his job was safe given that Pat Riley, the team's general manager and Spo's mentor, had full faith in him. That allowed Spo to keep his eye on the long game.

That doesn't happen at a lot of places. When things aren't going well, the coach is usually the one twisting in the wind. The Heat wouldn't have survived those early months without a strong culture set in place by Micky Arison, the owner, and Pat Riley, the GM. It's why the Heat remained competitive even after LeBron left. Spoelstra is still the head coach, and Riley is still the team president. In a league where constant change is the norm, the Heat are a notable exception.

Another guy I've been impressed with is Rob Pelinka, who's now the general manager of the Lakers. Like Bob Myers, Rob is a former agent (Kobe Bryant was his biggest client), so he understands the business from a different perspective. He has only been in that job since February 2017, but the Lakers have drafted very well. In one draft class, they got Lonzo Ball and Kyle Kuzma in the first round, and Josh Hart in the second. Drafting well with multiple picks isn't just about adding good players to your roster, it's about adding assets that could be valuable on the trade market.

When it comes to connecting with fans, there aren't many franchises that compare to the Oklahoma City Thunder. It's a young franchise in a small city, but they make it work. Besides being around the team so much because of Russell and KD, I also go way back with the Thunder's assistant general manager, Troy Weaver. He was an assistant coach at Syracuse when I was a walk-on there. Like Golden State, OKC has done an outstanding job building its roster through the draft. This is the team that drafted Durant, Westbrook, James Harden, Serge Ibaka, and Steven Adams. Not bad. They also hired two really good coaches in Scott Brooks and Billy Donovan.

I'm not surprised that Billy has, like Brad Stevens, made a smooth transition from college to the NBA. I worked with a bunch of Billy's former players at Florida, and in the off-season they'd fly to Gainesville so he could work them out. He still works out his own players as the head coach of the Thunder. That struck me because most head coaches don't do that. I thought it was Billy's way of letting his players know he didn't think he was bigger than the team. He could have sent out an assistant coach or a player development guy, but he wanted to do it himself. Billy used to play for Rick Pitino, and he coached under him for a little while with the Knicks. Billy was the ultimate gym rat, and becoming a head coach in the NBA didn't change that.

When you think of great NBA cultures, the San Antonio Spurs also leap to mind. I had a cool experience in early 2018 when the team's general manager, R. C. Buford, invited me to visit so he could pick my brain about player development. R.C. asked me to meet him at Texas A&M on a day the Aggies were playing a home game against Arkansas. I'd met him before, but we'd never spoken for more than ten minutes. We talked all through the game, and then we talked for another two and a half hours on the drive back to San Antonio. He dropped me off at a hotel and picked me up the next morning at eight o'clock. Most teams would send an assistant or an intern to do that. R.C. drove us to the Spurs' practice facility and we talked there for more than an hour.

The next thing we did was go to practice. I'd worked in the past with Pau Gasol, and we'd talked about the Spurs and the manner in which Gregg Popovich runs things. He quoted one of Pop's favorite sayings: "There's no fake hustle here." The players and the coaches all work hard, but the culture is based on individual accountability. You come in, you get your work done, and then you get out of there. They're not trying to impress anyone by requiring people to be there at all hours of the day. It's just an environment of pure professionalism.

After the practice some of the younger guys played a little pickup. On the day I was there, Tim Duncan joined

them. It was awesome to see one of the all-time greats showing the younger guys his old tricks, but it also spoke to the
environment that R.C. and Pop have helped create. Tim
was retired, but he still felt like he was part of the family.

I realize Pop is one of those old-school guys who'll rip
his players pretty good, but he's earned that respect. He
also spends enough time with his players away from the
court so they know where he's coming from. Pop goes
after everyone, man. I've seen him get on Duncan, Manu
Ginóbili, and Tony Parker as much as the guys coming off
the bench. He holds everyone to the same standard. You
can't fake that. Pop has a good way about him, too. He can
rip a guy to shreds, but a moment later crack a funny joke.
A little humor goes a long way in this business.

✕   ✕   ✕

Fans only see the glamorous parts of being in the NBA,
but even for the best players it's a stressful life. First, the
season is eighty-two games. Human bodies aren't built for
that kind of pounding. That's why a lot of these teams use
sleep specialists now. Rest and recovery are at a premium.
And once you go beyond the top five or six players on
each team, the other half of the roster is just one injury or
draft pick from being out of a job. These guys often have
extended families to support, and they age real fast. I've
seen too many friends get hurt during a contract year. It
can be devastating way beyond the physical part.

Over the years I've come to appreciate just how hard it
is to make the NBA, even for guys who were really good
in college. We know about the superstars, but the majority
of the rosters are filled with players who bounce around

from team to team, and who shuffle into and out of the NBA over a number or years.

Trey Thompkins is a good example. He averaged sixteen points and eight rebounds per game as a six-foot-ten forward at Georgia, and in 2011 he was signed by the Clippers as an undrafted free agent. He made the team, but after his second year the team declined to re-sign him. I ran Trey's predraft workouts and I thought he had a chance to be a good pro. He eventually decided he could make more money overseas. He's currently playing in Spain. I know that's a hard decision for players because the dream of making the NBA is so strong. It's especially challenging for players who've gotten a taste of the NBA life. When you're playing overseas, you're not coddled with private jets and luxurious hotels. You probably don't speak the native language, and most leagues only allow two Americans per squad. But for guys like Thompkins it can be a really good option.

For the ones who do make it to the league and stay there, it's very important that they don't get too caught up in the NBA life. The parties, the money, the women, the celebrity temptations—these things have been around for a long time, but now there's so much more of everything, and of course social media inflames it all. There are so many more opportunities for guys to get involved in outside business interests. Take the whole fashion thing, for example. Russ has been very active in that space. Guys are making statements just by how they choose to dress as they walk into the arena on game night (although frankly, I'm not a big fan of the suit shorts).

The scary part is how much younger players are nowadays when they get all these perks thrown at them. I can't imagine being Jayson Tatum and coming into the league at nineteen years old to be the man for a marquee team like the Boston Celtics. When I was nineteen, I was hanging in a dorm with my friends. I did plenty of dumb stuff, but for someone like Tatum, one wrong move or one wrong tweet and you can get buried.

I've had enough wild experiences being out with NBA players to get a small taste of what they deal with. I remember taking a trip with Kevin Durant to Europe in September 2013. We were in Rome and went to dinner with some folks. After dinner someone suggested we go out for a drink, and somehow we found ourselves in this little dive bar in the middle of Rome. It was almost like a college bar, but KD being seven feet tall, it was really easy to notice him. We didn't stay long, but when we left, there was a huge sea of people just waiting to get a glimpse. As we walked down the street, a huge crowd followed like a gallery behind Tiger Woods. KD is generally a friendly guy and pretty comfortable in these situations, but that one got out of hand real quick.

It's amazing how popular these guys are around the world. I remember one time I was in China with Derrick Rose. We showed up at an outdoor court and surprised the kids who were playing. This was the summer after he won MVP, so he was at the height of his popularity. Derrick walked up to the court and said, "We got next." So Derrick, his friend Randall, and I end up playing these random Chinese kids in three on three. Next thing you know, there were several hundred people surrounding the court and cheering. Word got out fast, as it usually does. That's life in the NBA.

✕ ✕ ✕

It's not easy for an older player to decide between making more money or signing with a team that gives him a chance to win. I know these guys get paid a lot regardless, but remember, most are done in their early thirties—if they're lucky. That leaves a lot of years to cover your monthly rent after you retire. Yet at the same time, as they see their careers winding down, it can be dispiriting if they've never had a chance to win a championship. I remember thinking about that when Karl Malone and Gary Payton came to the Lakers. They didn't get that long-elusive title, but they took their best shot and got to the Finals.

More recently, DeMarcus Cousins accepted less money to sign with the Warriors, and he's not that old. If you're going to do that, you better be ready to check your ego at the door. You see some older guys who've accomplished a lot in the NBA having to cede playing time to guys who are a lot younger. But if it leads to a title, then it's worth it.

I don't mean to sound cynical, but my advice to these guys is to make money a very high priority. I was pretty amazed when David West turned down $11 million from the Pacers to sign with the Spurs for $1.5 million. He didn't win a title in San Antonio, but a year later he won one with the Warriors. Winning was that important to him.

It's not easy for someone who has been in the NBA to transition into his postplaying life. The first revelation that hits is that you're not earning the money you used to. A lot of these guys have friends and family on their payroll and they have to let them know that that's no longer the case. They're still young men and they're not really qualified to do anything else. They think it's going to be easy to just hop on a coaching staff, but it's not, and even if you get a job you have to work your way up, starting with very little salary.

And of course, the hardest part is the inability to replace that thrill of competition. Once you've played in front of twenty thousand screaming fans, nothing ever comes close. Not to mention missing the camaraderie of a locker room and traveling with your friends and teammates. A lot of guys can't handle having to live without that. I get contacted by a lot of former players who just want to be around the game. They want to come with me to the arena, or help me work out other guys, just to feel that they're still a part of it.

*   *   *

My wheelhouse, of course, is the draft. Of all the aspects of running an NBA franchise, that's the area where I've been most involved. My main takeaway is how big a factor luck is. These players are coming into the league at such a young age, which means the teams have watched them less, so it's harder to project how much they'll improve. That's why mistakes get made. Look at Giannis Antetokounmpo. He's one of the truly elite players in the NBA, but he went fifteenth in the 2013 draft. I saw some video of Giannis in the run-up to that draft and had conversations about him with people all around the league. Believe me, no one saw this coming.

On the flip side, Markelle Fultz had all kinds of problems in Philadelphia. Nobody should rip the Sixers' front office for that. Almost every team would have taken Fultz as the first pick that year, or at the very least in the top two or three. Donovan Mitchell went thirteenth in the 2017 draft and was the runner-up for rookie of the year. For every Kwame Brown or Michael Olowakandi who gets picked high and doesn't pan out, there are a bunch of players like

Carlos Boozer, Draymond Green, Nick Van Exel, and Isiah Thomas who go in the second round and flourish. There are a lot of smart people who run NBA teams, and most passed on those guys when they were drafting.

Sure, NBA teams get to watch prospects work out in the weeks prior to the draft, but a lot of those sessions are solo and don't involve contact, so they don't tell you much. And since many workouts are run by agents, they're designed to showcase the players' strengths and minimize their deficiencies. Trust me, I know. The agents have a lot of say in how this all goes down. Sometimes an agent might want his client to get drafted a little lower so he ends up with a team that better fits the player. Teams want to stay on good terms with the most powerful agents because they don't want to do anything to jeopardize their ability to do business with their clients.

The other aspect that makes drafting extremely difficult is the difference between college and the pros. You see so many guys who are great in college—Jimmer Fredette and Adam Morrison come to mind—but don't stick in the NBA. Contrast that with Dion Waiters, who came off the bench at Syracuse and was a top-five pick and is doing great. The growing international pool is another challenge for evaluators. I thought Danilo Gallinari would be an okay pro, but I didn't anticipate how well his talents in Europe would translate to the NBA. The knock on him was that he was soft and didn't want to play defense, but when I worked him out, I saw a very competitive side that surprised me. People were questioning Luka Dončić even though he's one of Europe's best young players ever. He got picked third by the Hawks, who then traded him to the Mavericks for Trae Young. But it was Dončić, not Young, who put together one of the best rookie seasons in NBA history.

All this guesswork is why teams dig so deeply into a player's background. They'll talk to former coaches, teachers, family friends, other students they hung out with at school—anything to turn up a tiny little nugget of information that will help them make a smarter choice on draft night. The teams conduct extensive interviews with draft prospects at the combine or during separate visits. My advice to the players I work out is always the same: Tell the truth. Because if a team is asking you a question, there's a very good chance they already know the answer.

When a player doesn't pan out in the league, people tend to say he was drafted too high, but often the more important factor is what teams do with their players *after* the draft. The players at the very top are usually going to succeed no matter what, but beyond that, a lot depends on how a team develops that player and whether the roster makeup, as well as the coach's style, are good fits. There are plenty of examples—Chauncey Billups comes to mind—who bounced around to a number of teams before enjoying a high level of success. We want players to be so good so soon that we forget how long it can take sometimes, especially since most come into the league before they're old enough to drink.

There's no doubt that some teams draft better than others, but there's really no secret to evaluating prospects. You've got to get out there and see these kids play in person and up close as much as you can. A lot of general managers like to delegate this to their scouting staffs, and I realize their first responsibility is to their own teams. But if a team's decision makers aren't at games watching prospects, they'll tend to place too much emphasis on the workouts right before the draft. Workouts are another helpful data point, but they're not nearly as important as watching with your own eyes a kid play in a big, competitive game.

One value the predraft workouts do have is they let teams know what kind of work ethic a guy has. The players have time between the end of the college season and those sessions to work really hard on their bodies. Often, a guy will move up a few spots just by dropping a lot of weight, or gaining a lot of muscle, when he shows up for a team workout. If I were evaluating prospects, I'd definitely favor guys who prove they can work hard and get better.

Another mistake teams tend to make is overvaluing all the measurements and combine stuff. Again, these are good tools, but they're not as significant as the basic question: Can he play? I remember when people wondered about Kevin Durant's strength because he couldn't do a lot of reps with the 185-pound bench press. People also questioned whether Steph and Kristaps Porzingis were strong enough. These days, is anyone worrying about what those guys can lift?

*   *   *

When I first broke into this business, there weren't a lot of people training professional basketball players. Now, there are so many popping up that it's hard to keep track of them. I see pictures and videos of NBA players working out being posted all summer on social media. Some of it is pretty cool, but a lot of it cracks me up. I saw a video recently of a trainer throwing a player alley-oops that the guy had to catch while jumping over a mat. It looked ridiculous. Unfortunately, a lot of parents buy into that. They think because it looks different it's going to help. The problem is, a lot of that stuff has nothing to do with what happens in an actual game. It's a waste of time and money.

One of the funniest videos I ever saw was made by Damian Lillard. Someone had written to him over Instagram asking why he never posted images of himself working out. Wasn't he trying to get better? So Damian filmed this parody of him trying to dribble two basketballs while someone shot a Nerf gun at him. His point was, just because he wasn't putting his stuff out there didn't mean he wasn't doing his net work. That's why I give my clients free rein to post stuff on their own, but almost never do it myself. I want to protect their privacy, and besides, why tip off the competition about what you're working on?

*   *   *

A franchise's culture begins at the very top, but NBA owners are a tricky bunch. A lot are more involved in basketball decisions than fans realize. To be honest, I'm not sure that's a good thing. The owner is one of the *least* qualified people in the front office to make basketball decisions, but if the GM or coach doesn't listen to the owner he might get fired. I've heard of multiple instances where the owner overruled his basketball guys when it came to the draft. The best thing an owner can do is hire good basketball people and let them do their jobs without having to worry about looking over their shoulders.

I've also gotten to know a lot of agents, and my takeaway is the same as it is for everyone else: The best ones are honest with their clients. That's especially true when an agent is trying to convince a player to sign with him. I've seen too many agents overpromise in order to land a player, but then, when they don't deliver either money or playing opportunities, get fired pretty quickly. Worse, word will spread that the agent isn't trustworthy. It's crucial that an agent communicate well and visit with his players often. Players like to know they have their agent's attention.

As the number of outside basketball trainers has increased, I find that teams are getting more wary of letting outsiders penetrate their organizations. Fortunately, I have enough long-term relationships that I'm able to navigate the new terrain.

It's truly fascinating to watch the NBA operate from the inside, and then use what I've learned to do a better job for my clients and build out my business. I'd be lying if I said I hadn't thought about working for a team, and maybe even running one someday. I imagine that it would be stressful, but also a lot of fun. Same thing for the idea of being on an NBA bench. I don't think I'd like to be a head coach, but it would suit me well to be a player development guy. One thing I know for sure, doing net work with the best players in the world is a pretty great way to make a living.

CHAPTER ELEVEN

TWELVE RULES FOR BECOMING A BALLER

I still train kids of all ages, from eight years old to seniors in high school and beyond. I also do about a half dozen clinics per year where fifty or so kids show up. It's a nice addition to my business, yes, but mostly I do it because I started out working with young players, and I still really enjoy it. I'm not talking about future pros, or even future college players. I'd never limit myself in that way. If you love to hoop and you're willing to work, I'm happy to get out there and help you get better.

I love working with young kids because they don't have a lot of bad habits. They're there mostly for the fun of it and to get some exercise. True, most of the families who hire me are well off, but I don't see a lot of parents who have unrealistic expectations for their kids. They just want to see their sons and daughters work hard, show some discipline, and stay humble. For example, I work with two grandsons of Peter Guber, one of the owners of the Warriors. Their parents know the boys aren't going to play in the NBA, but they were very clear that if they were going to pay to fly me out to L.A. to spend a week training them, then the boys would have to commit. They wouldn't be allowed to bail at the last minute because they were too tired or wanted to play Fortnite. The kids have stuck to that deal.

I've also trained the sons of Disney CEO Bob Iger. I worked with his older son, Max, when he was in high school, and I still work out his younger son, Will. When we're done with our sessions and I'm on a court where I'm training my NBA guys, Will likes to stay around and rebound. It's pretty cool to see a kid who has grown up in that kind of lifestyle wanting to spend six or seven more hours in the gym just because he loves basketball.

When a parent asks me how I'm going to train their son or daughter, my answer is, "The same way I train the pros." Obviously, the performance level will be different, but the essence of working hard to get better remains the same. It's all about effort, fundamentals, details, persistence, and getting those perfect reps.

The most important thing for me is to make sure the kids are serious about doing their net work. They need to know we're not going to be playing HORSE all day. I'll send them the same video clips I send to my NBA clients, just to assign a little homework and make sure they're paying attention. I'm not as aggressive with kids as I am with many of my NBA guys, but on a few occasions when I didn't think the player was sufficiently committed, I let him and the parents know they were wasting their time and mine. I'm as honest with them as I am with the pros.

My own kids are still toddlers, but my involvement with other young players has exposed me to the world of youth sports in America. It's not a pretty sight. Parents are a lot more involved at all levels. I like seeing parents connected to their kids' lives, but the whole thing has gone way overboard, in my opinion. The stakes are getting higher all around, which means more of everything.

It seems to me that there's not enough player development going on at the high school level. I realize coaches have limited time and don't get paid much, but what's the sense in teaching your players offensive sets that put them in position to score if they don't know *how* to score? There's a difference between teaching and coaching. I'd like to see more teaching and less coaching in high school and younger.

The problem is even greater in grassroots ball—CYO, travel, AAU, summer tournaments, or anything else besides high school ball. There's a lot of emphasis on being flashy. Unfortunately, fundamentals don't get you on a mixtape or attract views on YouTube. Dunks and effective crossovers are the main currency there. When Zion Williamson was in high school, no one knew whether he could shoot, pass, or dribble because all we saw were clips of him dunking. Who wants to watch a high school player doing a one-dribble pull-up? That's an important part of the game, but it takes time and effort to learn to do it properly and consistently. I'm not sure how many players are committed in that way.

Another problem with grassroots ball is the sheer *number* of games everyone plays. I've never understood it. These kids might play five games in the course of a long weekend. Even NBA players don't do that. Then there's the huge expense and travel time involved in competing in elite tournaments around the country. Is that really a good investment? As a parent, I'd want to make sure my kid learns the game. Are these teams working on basic chest passes and midrange pull-ups? I know there are a lot of positives to grassroots ball, especially the exposure a player can get for potential scholarships, but with so many teams playing so many games, the quality of the experience is diminished.

For those of you who aspire to make this great game an even bigger part of your life, I've put together this handy guide that is equally useful whether you're a kid or a parent. It's my Twelve Rules for Becoming a Baller. Success is never guaranteed, of course, in basketball or in life. But if you apply yourself and follow these rules, you'll be giving yourself the maximum opportunity to live out your dreams.

For purposes of clarity I'm using male pronouns, but obviously these rules apply to women as well. A baller is a baller.

RULE ONE: DON'T SHOOT

Not at first, anyway. When I was coming up in the game, it seemed everyone wanted to dunk. Nowadays, it's all about the three-pointer. This can be a huge problem for a player who's just starting out, especially if he's real young, because it leads to the creation of bad habits. I mean, there's no way for a kid that size to maintain proper form if he's shooting from behind the three-point line. The only way for him to reach the rim is to shoot from the hips. If he does that, when he gets older he'll have to relearn how to shoot the ball the proper way, with the wrist cocked and the elbow underneath the ball. It's not worth it.

When I'm working with an eight-year-old, we do mostly ball-handling and footwork drills. Of course, the kids all want to shoot at that age—at any age, really—but I won't let them launch from outside of the paint. I tell all my clients, including the NBA players, that basketball starts with the feet. So when a player is real young, that's what he needs to work on. The shooting will come eventually, but there's no rush.

If you're the parent of a young player, encourage him to keep a ball in his hands at all times. As I write this, my son isn't yet four years old. We have a Nerf hoop in the house and he likes to hold the ball as he walks around. At that age, you just want your child to be curious about the game and comfortable with a ball in his hands. Even if he's just watching TV at home, having a ball in his lap will give him a head start on becoming a baller. Learning bad shooting, on the other hand, is a surefire way to set him back.

RULE TWO: KEEP BEEF IN YOUR DIET

When you do start to work on your shooting, remember the BEEF. That stands for Balance, Eyes, Elbow, Follow-through.

First and foremost, shooting starts from the ground up. The feet need to be properly spaced and facing the hoop. The player should be in balance not only when he attempts his shot, but also when he lands. As you get older the shots may be more creative, with fallaways and runners and floaters and the like, but the fundamental of a jump shot is to start and end in balance.

Second, the eyes should be on the back rim—not the front, not the middle of the net, but the back. As I wrote earlier, if you miss a shot, you should miss it long. The best way to do that is to lock your eyes on that back rim when you release the ball. When a parent or coach takes a player to the playground, he should pay attention to where the ball caroms off the misses. If the ball is going back directly at the player, then he's headed in the right direction as a shooter.

Then there's the elbow. It should always be underneath the ball, like a waiter carrying a tray of food through a restaurant. Most kids want to pop that elbow out to the side to get more arm strength into the shot. That means they are shooting from too far away.

Finally, the follow-through. It should be the same every time, no matter how the rest of the body is postured. The wrist and fingers should flick as the ball is released. If you're picturing a clock, shoot the ball right at eleven o'clock. It is important to groove this follow-through into your shooting motion. That means lots and lots of perfect reps to build muscle memory.

RULE THREE: DON'T HAVE A POSITION

When I first start working with a young kid, I'll ask him what position he plays. Whatever his answer, I'll let him know that I'm not buying it. "You're not a shooting guard, you're a *player*. You're too young to define yourself with a position." To me, that's an unnecessary limitation. I don't care how big you are. You need to learn to shoot, dribble, and pass just like everyone else.

This is something more and more young players and their families are understanding at the outset. It used to be that a bigger kid was automatically stationed near the basket. Problem is, a lot of times the kid is just an early bloomer. By the time he gets to high school, his buddies have caught up and he's the same size as everyone—but he doesn't have nearly the same skill set.

On the other hand, it's common to see a player develop guard skills when he's young and then grow real late. Once he gets that combination set, he becomes a big-time player.

This has become true all the way through to the NBA. As I've detailed in earlier chapters, there really are not many traditional back-to-the-basket post players anymore. I always work with my big men on their shooting, and I try to teach smaller players how to post up and rebound. The more versatile you are, the better chance you have to contribute to your team. Specialists don't make nearly as much impact as they used to. So from the very start, don't think of yourself as having a position. As the saying goes, there are really only two positions in basketball—on the court, and off the court.

RULE FOUR: WORK ON YOUR STRENGTHS

A lot of coaches and trainers will insist that their players spend a lot of time working on weaknesses. Not me. I'm all for shoring those up and adding facets to your game that aren't there, but I'm still a believer that the best way to advance as a baller is to get better at the things you do best. When Steph Curry comes into my gym, do we work on post-up moves? Of course not. We shoot a ton of threes. I don't care if he made 55 percent during the season. I'd like to see if we can get that up to 57 or 58.

One reason to work on your strengths is that if you don't keep your skills sharp, you'll surely regress. You can never just lock in a skill and put it on the shelf so you can do other things. If you're a great post scorer and you spend your whole summer working on face-up midrange jumpers, when it's time to get back on the blocks you won't be effective. It's like what Ben Hogan used to say about golf. He felt that if he missed one day of practice it took two days to make up for it. You've got to keep that muscle memory sharp, especially when it comes to the parts of your game that helped you get where you are.

I'll never forget going to Michael Jordan's camp and hearing him say, "You're never a finished product. You can always get better." If that's true for the GOAT, it's definitely true for you. Don't assume that just because you're really good at one aspect of the game, that's the best you can do. You should always be trying to get better.

RULE FIVE: MOVE FORWARD

I often tell players that the best reaction is no reaction. If a guy misses five straight shots, I don't want to see his head go down. "Make the sixth," I'll say. The same is true if he makes five in a row. There's no need to be jumping around and celebrating. That won't help you make the sixth one, either.

It's very important for a player to keep his confidence no matter how bad things get. The only way to get there is by moving forward at all times. This is especially true for young kids. They tend to get caught up in what just happened, good or bad, instead of focusing their energy and attention on what's next. But to become a baller, you have to be able to transition to the next play right away, regardless of what happened on the last one.

RULE SIX: BE RESPECTFUL

This is a big one for me. I tell all the young players I work with who say they want scholarships, "Someone is always watching." If a kid is making an obnoxious face to a referee every time he gets called for a foul, or if he comes out of a game and kicks a chair because his teammates aren't passing to him, that will be observed, word will get around, and it could affect how he's recruited.

That's especially true today with social media and smartphones. Not only do you not know who's watching, you don't know who's recording and who's posting. If a young player does something wrong in a game at night, there's a chance that half of the college coaches in Division I will know by morning. Like I said before, everyone in basketball pretty much knows one another. If you're disrespectful, word will get around fast.

I'm amazed at how often I've seen players being disrespectful even when they *know* college coaches are in the gym. Coaches are literally putting their careers on the line when they're making decisions about whom to recruit. They're not just looking for good players, they're trying to maintain a certain culture. And they don't want disrespectful players.

I can be tough on the younger guys in this regard. If I see something in their facial expressions or body language that I don't like, I'll let them know. It's not just about respecting me, it's about respecting the game—and respecting themselves. "No offense," I'll say, "but I've worked with players who are a lot better than you, and I don't hear them complaining." Once in a great while I'll invite a kid to call his parents to pick him up, but I've never had a kid take me up on that one. Eventually, competitive pride kicks in.

A lot of top players tend to change high schools frequently these days. I'm all for chasing opportunity. Sometimes the players are moving to better academic schools and more competitive basketball programs. Too often, however, they're just looking for the path of least resistance so they can get more playing time right away. If a player changes schools, that's not a big deal. If he changes two or three times, that might make a college coach wonder, *Is it the schools that are the problem or the player?*

Unfortunately, this school-changing habit is often repeated at the college level. Again, I'm all for players moving around to find the right opportunities. After all, coaches do that all the time. But sometimes you have a situation where a player doesn't want to wait a year or two to get better and be ready when the opportunity to play presents itself. If he goes to a great program, there's a reason the school has been winning. There are good players there. When I was at Syracuse, there were guys on the team who were All-Americans in high school but didn't get quality minutes until their junior or senior seasons. The question is, are you capable of sticking it out and putting in the net work to get better?

RULE SEVEN: PICK THE RIGHT SYSTEM

If you're good enough to play in college, don't just pick a school because it has a known "brand" or an accomplished coach. Make sure that coach's system is suitable for you. This is where both the coach and the player make mistakes that lead to rampant transferring.

It's also important to have a genuine relationship with that coach, regardless of how many career wins he has. There's a good chance you're going to spend four or five years with him. That's a lot of hours of practices, games, and time spent on the road. Ideally, this is a relationship that is going to last a lifetime.

Parents should be involved in the recruiting process, but in the end it's very important to let the player make the decision. He's the one who's going to have to live with it, whether it works out or not. Plus, it's inevitable that he's going to encounter adversity. If the player thinks his parents pushed him in one direction, he won't be fully committed. And if things don't work out, he'll blame the parents instead of taking ownership.

RULE EIGHT: STUDY THE GAME

This was a huge part of my basketball education. No one had to assign it to me. If a game was on television, I was going to watch it. I didn't just watch it, either. I paid close attention to how the players were moving, how they were defending, the decisions they made, the way they got open, the way they shot the ball—anything that had to do with the game. I loved locking in on the smallest details, and I couldn't wait to try out what I learned on my friends.

Nowadays, it's much easier for young players to study the game. You can record every game on a DVR, and of course you can access everything online. You can go on YouTube and study the all-time greatest players. If you want to be good, and if that resource is available, why wouldn't you use it?

When I send a video clip to an NBA player, I try to keep it to about two to four minutes. I send them every ten games or so because I want to get a feel for what's happening. If they're going to be in the playoffs and facing a certain opponent, then I'll bump up the frequency. There's some critical stuff in there but a lot of positive reinforcement as well, and I try to make it relate to what we worked on in the summer. Or I'll ask them if they want to see anything in particular. Either way, I think video is a very important teaching tool, and it helps me stay connected to my clients during the season. I actually learn as much by watching all that video as by being with them in the gym.

I emphasize to all my players, professional and amateur, that there's a skill that goes into watching video. I've learned how to caption images to highlight specific things. Sometimes I'll send a guy a video of a *different* player to show him what I'm trying to get him to do. I always ask for feedback. If the player I'm working with doesn't respond or tell me what he thinks about the videos, I'll stop sending them. Even if a player disagrees with my analysis, I want to know about it.

When I send those video clips to my young players, I want to know what they think and what they see, but mostly I want them to start thinking of the game as something to *study*. Watching games isn't just entertainment, it's education. I also encourage them to watch video of themselves whenever possible. There are a lot of ways to study the game these days. A true baller uses all of them.

RULE NINE: SACRIFICE

When I come into my clinics, the first thing I do is praise the campers for being there. "It's nine in the morning on a Sunday," I'll say. "Your friends are sleeping or playing video games, or they're at the beach. But you're here. That's a good start. Showing up is the toughest part."

Look, it's up to you how good you want to be. Are you going to sit at home and play video games for four hours? Or are you going to find a gym and develop your fundamentals? Are you going to watch a Celtics game and study how Kyrie Irving gets open, or how Kevin Durant beats his guy off the dribble, or how Kevin Love fights his way for every rebound? The only way to be great at anything is to truly love it, and that requires sacrificing a lot of other things. Lots of kids have dreams about becoming a baller. The special ones know that the only way to get there is to work for it.

I know I'm going to sound like the old guy here, but when I was a senior in high school, my friends and I would get up early on the weekends to work out at the school gym. If the gym wasn't available, we played outside. It might be cold, it might be early, but we were there. When I coached at Bishop Hendricken, there were players willing to get up an hour before school started and work out in the gym with me. Sometimes the floor would be set up for an assembly, so we'd fold up all the chairs and put them to the side. When we were finished practicing, we had to put the chairs back.

So I ask all aspiring ballers, What's it going to take? Are you willing to make the sacrifices required to get good at this game? Or will you stop short when things get hard?

This rule applies at all levels. For the high school player, it means going to bed early on a weekend night because you have a game the next day, even though your pals are out partying and having a good time. In college, it means staying at school over the summer, missing Christmas and Thanksgiving vacations with your family, so you can get the edge on guys you're competing with for playing time. As a pro, it means being disciplined with your eating, maintaining your body, resisting the temptations of the wealthy celebrity's lifestyle. And as always, it means the willingness to put in your net work, even—or should I say especially— when you don't feel like it.

RULE TEN: BE A LEADER

A true baller doesn't just take care of himself. He lifts up his teammates. That's the great thing about basketball. No matter how good you are, you can't win big alone.

The older coaches will tell you that this generation of players—the "me" generation—is more focused on themselves than on being good teammates. I hope that's not true. I see a lot of young players trying to be leaders. There are a lot of things that go into that. First and foremost, you have to set a good example. You can't tell your teammates they need to act a certain way and then not follow up yourself. It's the same principle that applies to parents. Your kids will do as you do, not as you say.

Don't think you have to be the best player on the team to be a leader, either. To me, one of the best ways to be a leader is to accept a complementary role, or be willing to come off the bench. Often in college, a coach will need to take a senior out of the starting lineup for the benefit of the team. If the player sulks, it can kill the locker room. If the player buys in and embraces the change, the team can thrive. As the saying goes with ballers, "Real recognize real." If a guy is all about himself, the rest of the team and all the coaches will surely know it.

Every team needs leaders, from biddy basketball to the NBA. And being a leader doesn't always mean being the loudest guy in the locker room, either. There's no better example than Tim Duncan. When I visited San Antonio, R. C. Buford told me that in all the years he was there, Tim was never late for anything. He never talked back to the coaches, almost never said anything to the refs. He never worried who got the credit. He and Gregg Popovich created a culture that was totally about the team. That's the impact of strong leadership.

RULE ELEVEN: VALUE WINNING ABOVE ALL ELSE

This rule seems obvious, but I'm amazed how often it isn't followed. On the one hand, I get it. Players have individual goals. The problem arises when the player thinks the way to reach those is to focus on the short term. The bottom line is, if the team is winning, then everyone benefits.

I remember watching Jason Hart fight through this during his senior year at Syracuse. The star of that squad was Etan Thomas, and a lot of players wouldn't have been happy playing a complementary role. Jason wasn't a naturally gifted offensive player, but he bought into his role because he knew it would help the team win—and that, in turn, would help Jason in his quest to make the NBA. Jason was the team's second-leading scorer and almost never came out, and although he was a late second-round pick, because he came from a winning program he ended up playing ten years in the league. Everyone knew he was a winner.

On the other hand, you may be one of those high school players who scores a ton of points, but if the team has a mediocre record, that could indicate to college recruiters that you're more interested in scoring than winning. And believe me, there's nothing more important to a coach than winning. If you want to play for him, you better feel the same way.

RULE TWELVE: HAVE FUN

I see too many parents taking things too seriously, especially when the kids are young. Basketball should be a form of recreation, period. As the player gets older, the idea of making high-level teams becomes important, but even then a parent has to be careful about applying too much pressure. I've had plenty of kids I've worked with miss ten shots in a row, and they get real frustrated and don't want to work anymore. I try to assure them, "Don't worry, it's basketball, let's have fun." It's important that parents reinforce that message, or the kid will lose interest.

I go through similar conversations with my pros. When they get too frustrated, I am quick to remind them, "It's okay. You're still making a living playing basketball. You need to have fun." There's a fine line here. Yes, it's a business, but if it's too businesslike, then the player won't be able to approach the game with the enthusiasm—the child-like enthusiasm—that made him great in the first place.

The biggest mistake I see parents make is pushing their kids too much, especially when they're young. The important thing is to give them the opportunity to play, and then see how it goes. Sometimes I get the idea that parents are trying to live their dreams through their kids, instead of letting them chase their own dreams. A player usually starts to figure things out when he gets into high school. When I'm training a young player, I don't mind if a parent is in the gym once in a while, but I usually think the better option is for them to leave the gym and let the kid have his time with me.

Parents have to realize that their kids naturally want to please them. I can remember playing games when I was younger—I'd look into the stands after making a good play to make sure my dad approved. Your kids need to know you care, but you also know when to take a step back. It's okay to talk about a game or a workout, but eventually enough is enough. You don't have to talk about it every night at dinner or repeatedly turn it into a lengthy discussion. It's important to let your kids have their own experiences when it comes to sports.

The father of a sixteen-year-old player dropped his kid off with me one time and before leaving the gym said, "Here you go. My kid doesn't listen to me anymore." I thought that was pretty funny. That's a good reason to bring in an outside trainer or coach, to make sure your kid is getting advice he'll actually listen to. When most of us were teenagers we weren't seeking out a lot of advice from our parents.

Basketball is a simple game, and even with all the changes over the decades, the essence remains the same. If you give everything you have to the game—if you put in your net work—then the game will give more back to you than you could have ever imagined. That's the joy of becoming a baller.

CHAPTER TWELVE

BEST OF THE BEST

One of the great things about sports is the way it lends itself to passionate debate. There's nothing like a good sports argument, right? Everyone's an expert, everyone has an opinion, and everyone is absolutely certain they're correct.

As a hoops junkie, there's nothing I love more than to hang out in the gym, or be at dinner, or go to a game and debate hoops with my friends. If you want to start a spirited discussion, ask people to name their best this or their worst that. No hedging! Making lists and rankings forces people to come to decisions that can be very difficult. LeBron or Michael? Hakeem or Shaq? Phil or Red? You have to choose, and then the fun begins.

Since I've spent basically my entire life watching, studying, and talking about basketball, I figured I'd end the book with a list of my personal bests in several categories. I wanted to select among people I've actually seen, either on TV or in person, so my pool of candidates only goes back to the early 1980s. And yes, I *am* partial to people I know and have worked with. Then again, I'm very lucky that I've been able to know and work with the best of the best.

So here are my choices. You can disagree if you want. But you'll be wrong.

BEST SHOOTER: STEPHEN CURRY

When people talk about Steph as a shooter, they usually focus on his quick release and perfect form. To me, what makes him special is his footwork. I always say shooting starts from the ground up. That's why I tell my clients to do their work early. Steph always keeps his body low when he is moving without the ball. His knees are bent, his hips are down. As soon as he catches the ball, it's out of his hands. Even when he's running a dead sprint in transition, when he catches that ball he is ready to let it fly. All of that is what enables him to use that quick release to such lethal effect. He's not making those thirty-five-footers with his arms. He's making them with his legs.

Steph is obviously one of the greatest three-point shooters the game has ever seen. Even back when he was a sophomore at Davidson, he set an NCAA single-season record for most threes in a season. He has set the NBA regular-season record for made threes in three different seasons, and he's well on his way to being the career leader for made threes in league history.

One thing that doesn't get mentioned, though, is his free-throw shooting. That to me is the real hallmark of a great shooter. If I see a player not shooting threes but making a real high percentage from the foul line, I assume he could be a good three-point shooter if he put in the net work. Most players dream of having a season where they make 90 percent or better from the line. Steph is over 90 percent for his *career*. That includes his second year in the NBA, when he made 93.4 percent. That's almost inhuman.

I've heard the comments some in the media (including Mark Jackson, the former Warriors coach) have made that

Steph has "ruined" the game by making the three-point shot so cool. I wouldn't say he's ruined the game, but he has definitely changed it. When I was growing up, everyone wanted to dunk. Now every kid wants to be like Steph. In eight to ten years we're going to see some of the most incredible shooters coming into the league, kids who grew up during the Age of Steph. It's going to make basketball that much more fun to watch.

If you ever saw Steph's father, Dell, play then you can't be all that surprised his son turned out to be a great shooter. Dell had as pure a stroke as I've ever seen. There weren't many guards who were as big as he was (six-foot-four) who could shoot like that back when he played. His release was perfect but his guide hand didn't move. That's tough to do every single time. Dell didn't start off as a great shooter (he made just 28 percent as a rookie in 1986–87), but by later in his career he strung together several seasons where he was over 40 percent. Needless to say, he knew how to put in his net work—and his sons did a lot of watching.

It's interesting that Steph should be playing for Steve Kerr, who still holds the record for the highest career three-point percentage in NBA history at 45.4 percent. But Steve will be the first to tell you that when it comes to the pure act of shooting, Steph is better. Steve was great, don't get me wrong, but he could play in space while guys like Michael Jordan and Scottie Pippen (and later Tim Duncan and Tony Parker in San Antonio) were drawing the attention of defenses. Plus, he didn't have the array of moves Steph uses to shake free.

Kevin Durant is right there in terms of perfect shooting form. It's almost like people don't realize how pure it is because KD is so good at all the other aspects of the game, but he's a career 38 percent shooter from three, and he has also had a few seasons where he was about 40 percent. Pretty good for a seven-footer.

I grew up watching Larry Bird. He was the first big man to really use that three-point line. Now every big man in the NBA wants to do that. I also watched from courtside as the 1987 Providence team coached by Rick Pitino and featuring Billy Donovan and Delray Brooks made a surprise run to the Final Four. Pitino was the first college coach to really embrace the math of the three-point line. I can never remember him getting angry at a guy for taking an open shot.

Then there's Ray Allen. Talk about perfect form. It's one thing to have that great form, it's another to do it the same way every single time. Like Steph, Ray never lost confidence as a shooter. Even though Ray has the NBA record for made three-pointers (for now, anyway), I chose Steph as my Best of the Best because he takes tougher shots—and still makes them. His ball-handling is absolutely vicious.

Finally, while I'm on the topic of listing the best shooters I've ever seen, let me add a name that I bet you've never heard of: Jimmy Baron. I first met him when he was playing for Bishop Hendricken High School. No, he never made the NBA, so I guess it's silly to put him in the same category as Stephen Curry. But he was a pretty good player who still holds the Atlantic 10 record for most career three-pointers. Like Steph, Jimmy grew up around the game because of his dad, Jim Sr., who was a college assistant and head coach for four decades. I've worked Jimmy out many times over the years and he's become one of my best friends. I've also worked out Steph and many of the NBA's greatest shooters. I'm telling you, as a pure shooter, Jimmy is very much in their class.

BEST SCORER: KEVIN DURANT

First, there's an important distinction to be made between *shooter* and *scorer*. Shooting is a pure physical motion that should be repeated each time. Scoring is more of an art form where a player has to find different ways to get the ball in the basket. Scoring requires versatility and improvisation. Not all players who score a lot of points are necessarily great shooters, and there are plenty of really good shooters who are one-dimensional. If you can find someone who's really good at both, well, then you have something special.

It's hard to go against Michael Jordan here, and I'll admit to being biased toward KD because of our relationship. But I've never seen an NBA player who could score so many points in so many ways. KD is all of seven feet tall, so he has the ability to take any defender inside. And as I mentioned above, from a pure shooting standpoint he is as good as anyone who has ever played.

As for Michael, well, as prolific as he was as a scorer, the thing that really separated him from his peers was his competitiveness. If there's one thing that gives MJ the edge over LeBron or anyone else in the Great GOAT Debate (Greatest of All Time), it was his killer instinct when it came to crunch time. For the first half of his career, Jordan could score by elevating over his defenders. Remember when he beat the Cavaliers because Craig Ehlo couldn't hang in the air quite as long as he did? Toward the end of his career, however, and especially with his third and final phase with the Washington Wizards, Michael stayed on the ground longer, but he still scored a ton of points because he was so smart and so skilled. In the last two years of his career, when Michael was thirty-nine and forty years old, he still averaged more than twenty points per game. And keep in mind, this was back in the day where hand checking was not only allowed, it was a common defensive tactic. Can you imagine how many points MJ would have scored in today's game, where if you sneeze on a guy you're called for a foul?

I remember when I was at Michael's camp and he talked about winning an NBA scoring title. The highest average was right around thirty-two points per game. So by his math, that just meant getting eight points per quarter. No big deal, right? When I worked at Wasserman with one of Michael's former Bulls teammates, B. J. Armstrong, he used to joke that the rest of the players waited for Michael to get those first eight points, and then the rest could go ahead and hunt their own shots.

One guy who's going to get lost in the best scorer conversation is Carmelo Anthony. When he was in his prime, he was a lot like KD, someone who could score every which way, from post-ups to three-pointers to everything in between. Melo was terrific in transition or in the half-court.

People rarely mention Hakeem Olajuwon in the best scorers conversation, but I believe he was the most fundamentally sound post scoring center in history. He was also ahead of his time in his ability to step away from the basket. Hakeem could bring the ball out to eighteen feet, and if you tried to pressure him there he'd cross you over and make you look real bad.

BEST PLAYMAKER: MAGIC JOHNSON

Of course, this seems obvious now, but if you go back to the way Magic was covered at Michigan State, there was healthy skepticism regarding how his game would translate to the NBA. He wasn't a good outside shooter, and he was six-foot-nine. He wasn't real fast, and he couldn't jump very high. What position was he going to play in the pros? He couldn't be a point guard the way he was in college, right?

That's why *playmaker* is the perfect word to describe him. Magic wasn't a jet like John Wall, and he didn't get by people using an explosive first step like Russell Westbrook's. He was simply able to get where he wanted on the court using his size and efficiency. His body was never out of control. When he got to where he wanted to go, he used his best asset—his mind. In fact, I'd argue that Magic is the smartest athlete in the history of sports. He made plays for his teammates like no one else in the history of the NBA.

Jason Kidd has to be on the short list as well. The guy had astounding court vision. He was the Russell Westbrook of his day, getting triple doubles on a regular basis. I'm a fan of big, strong guards because they can overpower defenders once they get in the lane. Like Magic, Kidd wasn't much of a shooter coming out of college. As a rookie, he shot 27 percent from the three-point line, but he ended up shooting 35 percent for his career and retired in ninth place on the all-time made threes list. His improved shooting made him that much more effective as a playmaker, because he'd learned to make plays for himself as well.

Guys like Kidd and Magic are special because of their court vision. I don't know if that's something that can be taught. That's just an innate talent. I do, however, instruct my clients that a great passer is always looking at the rim. That helps you see the whole floor. It also throws off the defense, like a quarterback in football looking one way to confuse the safeties and cornerbacks who are reading his eyes.

People might not think of John Stockton as a classic playmaker, but you have to be great at it if you're going to be the NBA's all-time leader in assists. Stockton's total of 15,806 is more than 3,000 better than the total of number two, Jason Kidd. (Stockton is also the all-time leader in steals, by the way. How many people know that?) Obviously, it helps to play with Karl Malone, who's second on the all-time scoring list behind only Kareem Abdul-Jabbar. Stockton wasn't super flashy like Magic, but he almost always made the right pass and the right play. He had a great feel for the game and the system he played in.

BEST DEFENDER: DENNIS RODMAN

We all think of Rodman as a great rebounder, but that's only part of what made him the best defender. He was so friggin' athletic and competitive. He could body up with a center, but he could also switch out on a point guard. That's why he was named to the NBA's all-defensive team seven times.

People have wondered whether Rodman might be less valuable in today's game given the premium on outside shooting. It's true he wouldn't be able to play that role on offense, but he'd still be very valuable on the offensive boards. I'd argue that he'd be even more effective as a rebounder because there's much more space underneath the rim now. But it's on defense where Rodman would make his mark if he were playing today. Because of all the screens that take place outside the three-point line, the ability to guard multiple defenders has never been more valuable. You could switch Rodman onto any player in this league, and he'd be the best defender that person has faced.

To be a great on-ball defender you have to have great hands, and nobody had a better pair of mitts than Gary

Payton. There's a reason they called him The Glove. Once he slipped himself onto a defender, there was no shaking him. Gary had the quickest hands I've ever seen. I also love that he took pride in his defense. He wanted to pick up guys full-court because he knew eventually it would wear them down physically and mentally. He was totally aggravating. You don't see that kind of dedication to defense in the NBA anymore. It's a scorer's league now.

BEST TEAMMATE: MANU GINÓBILI

When have you ever heard of a future Hall of Famer coming off the bench? That's what Ginóbili did over the last seven years of his career. He was good enough at that point to start for any other team in the league. Yet, he didn't ask for a trade, didn't complain to the coaches or the media, never walked out of practices or threw a hissy fit. He just made baskets, passed often, and played as hard as he could for his teammates. He understood that it's not important whether you start the game. What matters is whether you finish—and he finished most of them. I'm not sure we'll ever see something like that again.

As a player, Ginóbili was a sneaky good athlete. He was a great example of why slow-is-quick works in the NBA. He didn't show a lot of quickness, but before you knew it, he'd drive by you and dunk over the defenders. He was always changing pace and direction, so you never knew where he was going to go. He'd keep you guessing and then *boom*, he was by you. As time went on, his jump shot improved, which made the guessing game that much more difficult. He was the perfect guy to come off the bench because he could get quick buckets right away.

To me, Ginóbili was an extension of the Spurs' culture that owes a lot to David Robinson. He was one of the best players in the NBA when the Spurs drafted Tim Duncan in 1997. By the time Duncan got there, Robinson had already played in six All-Star Games. Did you ever hear him complain about having to share the spotlight with the rookie?

Of course not. In fact, the opposite happened. He mentored Duncan, deferred to him when necessary, and made sure Duncan had the best chance to succeed. Believe me, a lot of guys in Robinson's position wouldn't have been like that. It takes a lot of ego to get to that stage, but Robinson was able to put that aside for the sake of the team. As a result, the Spurs were able to win two NBA titles with Robinson and Duncan.

I touched on this earlier, but Kevin Love deserves a lot of credit for the type of teammate he was in Cleveland. Remember, he once had a night in Minnesota where he scored thirty points and pulled down thirty rebounds. When he went to the Cavs, not only did Kevin accept a lesser role next to LeBron, but he changed his game to become more of a pick-and-pop spacer. And because he was the new guy, every time the team went through a little bump in the road, he was the first to get blamed. Yet you never saw Kevin pop off to the media or put something on Twitter that caused a problem. Whatever issues were going on were settled in-house. We also now know that Kevin did all of this while dealing with mental health issues. Yet every day, he put his head down, came to work, and did everything in his power to help his team win. That's the definition of a great teammate.

One name that comes up often when I talk to players around the league about the best teammates is Kevin Garnett. From what I hear, he was great in that way on and off the court. He was very demanding of everyone, but that was only because he worked the hardest. His energy was off the charts. Whenever something bad happened, he was the first to take responsibility, whether it was really his fault or not. He treated everybody well around the organization. If he felt like someone on the other team was punking one of his guys, he would take up for him. I've heard stories about KG helping out low-level assistant coaches with their rent. To this day, he'll show up at practice with one of his former teams and offer encouragement to the guys who are there. So he's still being a great teammate.

If you want to go back in time a little bit, I'd give Joe Dumars a big nod here as well. Think of all the strong personality guys he played with on the Pistons—Isiah Thomas, Bill Laimbeer, Rick Mahorn, Dennis Rodman. Dumars was the one guy on that team who always kept his composure. And he could really shoot.

BEST ATHLETE: RUSSELL WESTBROOK

In a league that like no other puts a premium on pure athleticism, Russell truly stands alone. I don't believe we've ever seen a combination of speed, strength, elevation, and sheer determination like his. And yet, as I wrote earlier, his skill level isn't what separates him from the competition. You'd be hard pressed to find an example of someone who shoots so much and misses so often. Even so, he's perennially on the short list of MVP candidates. That's because of his athleticism.

When Derrick Rose was healthy, he could compete with anyone in this category. During his first few years in the league, Derrick would jump so high that he'd dunk the ball on his way *down*. I remember watching one of his early games in Chicago and one of the players threw Derrick an alley-oop on a fast break. He jumped up and flushed that thing with ease. I remember thinking, *This isn't the type of play you usually see from a point guard.*

I was born too late to watch Dr. J play in his prime, but the guy who stands out from my younger days is Dominique Wilkins. He wasn't one of those slender wings you usually saw get above the rim. He was a six-foot-eight power forward—and *power* was the exact right word. Dominique used to unleash these ridiculous windmills or reverse dunks where he brought the ball between his legs on the way up. Clyde Drexler was a great athlete, too, but he'd rather float over defenders. Dominique's purpose was to go *through* defenders and dunk on their heads. He was a great enough athlete to do it night after night.

BEST REBOUNDER: MOSES MALONE

Rodman is the easy answer here, so if that's your choice I won't argue, but from the pure ability to go up and get the ball, you can't do it any better than Moses did. I can't say whether he studied opponents' shots the way Rodman did, but he definitely had a feel about where he should await the miss. And Moses had maybe the strongest rebounding hands I've ever seen on an NBA player. When he got those things around the ball, there was no taking it away.

Getting a lot of rebounds isn't just about being tall. Nobody demonstrated that better than Charles Barkley. He came into the league as a six-foot-four power forward and he left sixteen years later with a career average of 11.7 boards per game. Height is one way for players to create space to get rebounds, but it's not the only one. There's vertical leap, which Barkley definitely had, but you can also create horizontal space as well. They didn't call Charles the Round Mound of Rebound for nothing. He used that big ole rump of his to move guys out of the way. The rest of it was just timing and pursuit. It all made for quite the compelling package.

BEST PLAYER DEVELOPMENT COACH: TIM GRGURICH

Most basketball fans don't know about Grgurich—or Grg, as he's known—but just about every coach in the league, as well as many in college, have benefited from his contributions in some way. Grg has spent most of his adult life conducting clinics for players and coaches. He runs a huge developmental clinic in Las Vegas each summer. Some of the best players in the world pay their own way and spend the week working with other great players and coaches to try to get a little bit better. Why don't you know about this? Because Grg doesn't let the media in to cover this event, and he steadfastly refuses to give any interviews. He's a true lifer—the coaches' coach.

He has been an assistant coach at several colleges and for many NBA teams, but aside from two brief stints at the University of Pittsburgh and UNLV, he was never a head coach. Wherever Grg has coached, he has put in a lot of hours on the side net working with players of all ages.

I first saw Grg do his thing with high school players at ABCD Camp. I knew that Mike Hopkins considered him a mentor, and I could really see the similarities. Grg was super intense. He was the only guy aside from Hopkins I've ever seen jump into drills, screaming and talking trash and playing some defense to amp things up. He even takes charges. That really showed me the way this net work stuff should be done. I never wanted to be a glorified passer. I wanted to be in the mix and make my players feel that they had a partner and teammate, not just a trainer.

In today's NBA, the guy who stands out to me is Chip Engelland. He was an undrafted player out of Duke who bounced around playing ball for a few years, mostly in Canada, before becoming an NBA assistant. Since 2005, he has worked for the San Antonio Spurs. Chip is known as a great shooting coach, but he's much more than that. I've seen a lot of players come to San Antonio and get better—guys like Tony Parker, Richard Jefferson, and Kawhi Leonard. It doesn't seem as if Chip has aspirations to be a head coach, which makes him unusual among NBA assistants. Plus, the Spurs really recognize his value. Every time someone tries to pry him away, they make it worth his while to stay.

MOST UNDERRATED: KEVIN McHALE

Kevin wasn't underrated just because he played with Larry Bird. It's because of *how* he played. He was all about footwork and fundamentals. He wasn't an elite athlete, not a dunker, not a three-point shooter. But when he had a defender on his back, the poor fella had no chance. Kevin had a million moves and counters, and he could finish with both hands. And of course, he was playing with Bird and a lot of other good players, so you couldn't give him too much defensive attention. Kevin was a very important part of a major sports dynasty, but you rarely hear him mentioned as one of the all-time greats.

In today's NBA, I would give my title of Most Underrated to Mike Conley of the Memphis Grizzlies. In his case, it's not his teammates who overshadow him but rather the other great guards in the Western Conference. Once you get past Stephen Curry, Russell Westbrook, James Harden, Chris Paul, and Damian Lillard, there's not a whole lot of oxygen left. It's amazing that in today's era Conley has played every season with the Grizzlies, who drafted him out of Ohio State in 2007. Conley has never made an All-Star team, but he did get the NBA's sportsmanship award twice. Everybody who plays with Conley raves about the guy. He's not the loudest player out there, but he leads by example, and he's a terrific teammate.

The people who do pay close attention to Conley know that he has an exquisite feel for the game. That's another thing you can't teach. He's never in a rush, doesn't turn the ball over a lot, knows how to play off ball screens, and is a great decision maker. He's not an explosive athlete like Russ, but he has a very quick first step. He's also a lefty, which makes him unconventional. And he's a winner. I don't know Conley well, but I did work him out for ten days during the summer of 2017. He showed up early, never missed a day, and did his net work like a pro.

BEST COACH: GREGG POPOVICH

If you're going to go strictly by number of championships, then Red Auerbach and Phil Jackson are the leaders of the NBA pack. I know every coach needs great players to win titles, and clearly Popovich has had a lot of great players, but I'm going with Pop here because he has done it for so long and with different kinds of teams and players, from David Robinson and Tim Duncan to Kawhi Leonard and Tony Parker. I think a lot of it has to do with the way he treats people. He doesn't really have a star system. Pop wants players who are going to add to the franchise's culture. That's a big reason why you don't get nearly as much drama with the Spurs as you see with other teams. Pop won't put up with it.

I didn't know Chuck Daly personally, but I'm still hearing stories about him from people around the NBA. When you hear the term *players' coach,* it's not always a compliment because sometimes it means the players are walking all over a guy. Chuck was a players' coach in a good way. There was never a question of who was in charge, and he certainly wasn't afraid to get on guys when they deserved it. But he was still able to come into the locker room and BS with everyone and bust chops like he was one of the fellas. Back then, a coach could go out and get a few drinks with his players without having to worry about someone posting it on social media. There's a thin line there, but Daly walked it as well as anyone. He also won two titles with the Bad Boy Pistons and was the head coach of the original Dream Team. So you know he knew his hoops.

Steve Kerr's job isn't as easy as a lot of people think. Yes, he has the best players, but that's a lot of egos and expectations to manage. Steve is very fiery and commands respect, but no one will ever accuse him of taking himself too seriously. Steve has lived an amazing life and is very thoughtful, and with all those championships he's the kind of guy who could write an amazing book. But he has said he wants to wait until he's through coaching because he doesn't want the attention to be on him. That's how you have to be to succeed in today's NBA.

Another guy who deserves a lot of credit as a great coach is Pat Riley. I like that he not only won with different teams, but won with different styles. His Showtime Lakers were a lot different from the physical, rugged teams he coached with the Knicks. Riley brought multiple titles to the Miami Heat, first as a coach with Shaquille O'Neal and Dwyane Wade and later as a GM with LeBron James. It's no coincidence that wherever Pat Riley has been, the wins have followed.

BEST ARENA: ORACLE ARENA

This is where the Warriors play, and while much of the environment can be tied to the team's winning ways, I spent a lot of time there before the Warriors took off, and I'm telling you it was still the best. Those are very loud, very passionate, very real fans. The place is always packed and the fans are ready to do their part. They're not just spectators—they're active participants in the game. The place sits in the heart of Silicon Valley, but it doesn't feel like a corporate environment the way so many other places do. If the team loses, the fans walk away genuinely upset. The energy on game nights is incredible.

I'd list the Thunder's home court, Chesapeake Energy Arena, as a close second. You get the same electricity as the games in Oracle, except Oklahoma City is much smaller than the Bay Area. There's a neighborhood feel when you watch a game in OKC. And once again, the fans are there to be heard, not just sit back and respectfully take it all in. It's always a treat for me to see a game there.

I used to love the old Boston Garden, but the Celtics' current arena, TD Garden, is still a great place to watch a game. The organization did an excellent job of re-creating the feel of their former place, right down to the parquet floor. And I'm here to testify that there is still no place on

Earth like Madison Square Garden. The history of that arena and that city comes through even when the team is struggling. The place just looks different—the lighting, the court, the layout of the seats. When you go to a game there, it feels like you're back in 1950.

Those fans are serious about their basketball, and they always show up. I was recently at MSG to watch the Knicks play the Suns. It was a random Monday night and they were two of the worst teams in the NBA, but every seat was filled and the joint was popping. I had to laugh and think to myself, *Only in New York.*

✳　　✳　　✳

I've been to more games at Madison Square Garden than I can count. I can't even guess the number of games I've seen in NBA arenas over the decades. And it's even harder to guess the amount of time I've spent in gyms and on blacktops, helping players of all ages, genders, and sizes reach their potential. The beauty of basketball lies in the variety. Whether you're Muggsy Bogues, who played at five-foot-three, or Manute Bol, who was seven-six, you can find a place as long as you're willing to put in the time and develop your craft.

That's the main thing I've learned during a lifetime spent in and around the game. If you think about it, there's really not that much difference between Oracle Arena and that court in the woods near my home in Rhode Island. Sure, the atmospherics are a little different, and there aren't as many people watching—but the rim still hangs ten feet off the ground. All the same rules and fundamentals of basketball hold true. That's what I hope you've learned in reading this book. Just like life, the game of basketball will reward you for what you put into it—but if you want the best results you have to commit, totally and completely. At the end of the day, it doesn't matter what court you're on. What matters is that you put in the work.

ACKNOWLEDGMENTS

Writing this book and revisiting all the stops in my basketball life have been both a pleasure and a privilege. I should point out that as *Net Work* was going to press, there was a flurry of trades and personnel moves that sent some of the people who are most prominent in this book to other teams—players like Derrick Rose, Al Horford, and Mike Conley, for example. Pro sports is always in flux, and the NBA, in particular, is. I'm just glad that my relationships with the people I've come to work with and respect have always stayed the same, even if the cities in which these friends are located frequently change.

As for those whom I want to specifically thank for helping me with this project, I'd like to express my gratitude to, first and foremost, Andrea Barzvi, my literary agent, and also Rick Horgan, my editor at Scribner, for believing in this project and helping to guide me through it. Kathleen Schmidt did me a huge favor in introducing me to Andrea. In many respects, I felt like a walk-on at Syracuse again, just hoping to earn a spot on the roster. From the very beginning Rick and Andrea were excellent teammates and coaches. This book also benefited from the work and attention of several others at Scribner, including Emily Greenwald, Dani Spencer, Brian Belfiglio, Nan Graham, and Colin Harrison. Thanks as well to my coauthor, Seth Davis, for putting my words to music.

My obsession with basketball was nurtured first by my parents, Bob and Jane McClanaghan. I don't know if it was because they just wanted me out of the house or what, but whenever I said I wanted to find someplace to dribble that ball, they were all about it. I know how proud they were when I did well. It's one of the main reasons I tried so hard.

I also played hard for my grandparents, John and May Lennon, and Robert and Catherine McClanaghan. My sister, Shana Gleason, has been my best friend and biggest supporter. I was and am very lucky to have great lifelong buddies in Brett Sylvia, Jimmy Baron, Dave Macari, Marcel Taillon, Kyle Rowley, Kris Stone, Ted Reidy, Ricky Esposito, and Angelo Simone.

I will forever owe a debt of gratitude to Steve Ceseretti, my coach at Bishop Hendricken High School in Warwick, Rhode Island. The best thing he did for me was *not* play me during my junior year. In doing so, he challenged me to put in my net work so I could play more as a senior. That summer is when I learned everything I needed to know about basketball. Thanks forever, Coach.

Speaking of great coaches, how can I ever repay the great Jim Boeheim? I had no business being anywhere near his practice court, yet he gave me an opportunity to show that I belonged. At Syracuse and ever since, Coach Boeheim has been a friend and mentor.

Three other coaches at Syracuse were instrumental in my development. Bernie Fine took me in and gave me confidence and always made me feel like I belonged. Mike Hopkins was the first person to show me what player development is all about. I'm not surprised that he's having such great success at the University of Washington. Troy Weaver, who's an assistant GM with the Thunder, has a great basketball mind and continues to be one of my best friends in the sport.

When I was unemployed and had no idea what I'd do next, Jamal Gomes, the head coach at Bishop Hendricken, gave me a break and hired me as his assistant coach and phys-ed teacher. He was very generous in letting me use his gymnasium to work out players and start making a name for myself. That was where I first started working with Ruben Garces and Ryan Gomes. I'm grateful that both of those players trusted me to work with them even though I was a total unknown at the time.

I still feel a little bad about burying Sonny Vaccaro under all those faxes, but with a push from his wife, Pam, he gave me a chance to work at his legendary ABCD Camp and sent me on my way. Thanks, Sonny.

Joe Abunassar was instrumental in getting my career launched as a player development trainer. He hired me at IMG Academy and gave me a full-time gig at IMPACT in Las Vegas.

What can I say about my Wasserman family? You guys discovered me, encouraged me, entrusted me, and empowered me. Thank you, forever and always, to Casey Wasserman, Arn Tellem, B. J. Armstrong, and Bob Myers.

The greatest compliment anyone can pay someone is to trust you with their kids. I'm grateful to the many hundreds of parents who've done just that over the years. I hope that besides teaching those kids a few fundamentals I fostered the love that these kids have for the great game of basketball.

In much the same fashion, I've benefited from the trust many NBA teams, general managers, and especially agents have placed in me over the years. They've given me access to some of the greatest players in the world. I feel very fortunate to consider myself a part of the NBA family. That closeness extends as well to the great folks at USA Basketball, especially Sean Ford, the men's national team director.

Special thanks go to the Jackson family for allowing me to use their home gymnasium in Los Angeles. It's a great place to get in some net work. Thanks, too, to media buddies Chris Mannix, Pete Thamel, and Adrian Wojnarowski.

As for all the NBA players I've trained . . . well, words fail me. (And as any of them can tell you, that doesn't happen often.) You've all given me more than just a great way to make a living. You've given me a wonderful life. And along the way, many of you have become some of my best friends. I'm reluctant to name names because I couldn't possibly list them all, but I must give special mention to Kevin Durant, Tyreke Evans, Al Horford, Brandon Jennings, Brook and Robin Lopez, Kevin Love, Chandler Parsons, Elfrid Payton, Derrick Rose, John Wall, and Russell Westbrook. (And yes, I listed them alphabetically so no one can accuse me of playing favorites.) Thanks, especially, to Stephen Curry—not only for letting me into his world but also for contributing the foreword to this book.

Finally, this book, like everything else in my life, is dedicated to my three amazing children, Ela, Gia, and Rob. I don't know what I did to deserve such great kids, but I do know that most of the credit goes to their mom, Daniela. Thanks to the four of you for all of your love and support.

INDEX

ABOUT THE AUTHOR

Rob McClanaghan is one of the NBA's most prominent and well-respected trainers. His clients include Stephen Curry, Kevin Durant, Tyreke Evans, Eric Gordon, Al Horford, Kevin Love, Candace Parker, Elfrid Payton, Derrick Rose, John Wall, Russell Westbrook, and countless others. *The Ringer* has called him "one of the most instrumental behind-the-scenes figures in basketball." He has also been featured in the *Washington Post* and *Sports Illustrated* and on Yahoo! McClanaghan attended Syracuse University, where he walked on to the basketball team, and was later employed by Wasserman Media Group to help its NBA clients prepare for the draft. He conducts several youth clinics and has produced numerous basketball instructional videos. McClanaghan has three children and lives in his native Rhode Island.